The
Choice

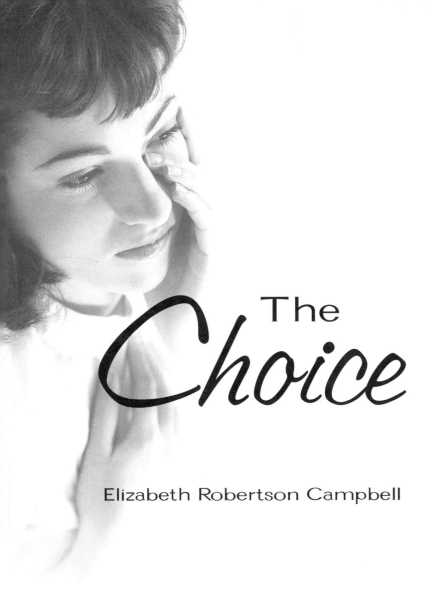

The
Choice

Elizabeth Robertson Campbell

Bridge-Logos

Orlando, Florida 32822

Bridge-Logos

Orlando, FL 32822 USA

The Choice
by Elizabeth Robertson Campbell

Copyright ©2006 by Bridge-Logos

Printed in the United States of America.

Library of Congress Catalog Card Number: 2006929229
International Standard Book Number 0-88270-228-9

G1.316.N.m607.35240

ACKNOWLEDGEMENTS

*I*t has taken me fourteen long years to put pen to paper, but I doubt that I would have done it if it were not for my countless wonderful friends and family members, who shared in my agony and ecstasy during the "Aaron" years. Thank you. Without all your dogged persistence, genuine love, and endless encouragement, I would never have succeeded.

I would also like to thank the many editors along the way (mostly friends) who so freely helped, spending their precious time correcting my foul spelling and grammar until Fiona came on board. Nothing can beat a professional, hand-picked from above, to bring everything together in a way far beyond my wildest dreams. A million thanks.

Debbie, a special word of thanks to you, my dear, for all your sacrificial consolation during one of the most devastating few days of my life, and also for coming up with the title of the book.

Then to you, too, Mom, thank you for buying me the computer which made this book possible. Then, even more, for the compassion you showed during my pain. (What would we do without loving mothers?)

Also, to Aaron, I want to thank him for all he taught me, and the unconditional love he showed during our life-changing time together. I will always honor you.

Last but not least, I thank my Creator for allowing me to learn these tough but priceless lessons about His people and Him. From this day onwards the prayer of Ruth will always be mine: "Your people will be my people and your God will be my God."

Thank you, one and all.

INTRODUCTION

Very few people can resist a good old-fashioned love story, especially when it ends well. This is the story of how I fell in love with a man, a country, and a city, and the obstacles we had to overcome.

Whether or not it has a fairy tale ending, you'll find out only if you read it from beginning to end.

Shakespeare would have been proud to come up with a plot like this one: a young South African artist goes to work in the International Christian Embassy in Jerusalem where she meets a fervent young Orthodox Jewish man, who has been taught to despise everything the young artist believes in.

It began when the young man (Aaron) decided to do something about this Christian presence in his community. Courageously he went to see "this place" for himself. When he arrived he found me, proudly sharing with all who visited how thousands upon thousands of Christians like myself had seen the light regarding Israel and God's plans for her. It was a topic Aaron was totally unprepared for and scoffed at any common ground I said we shared.

Stranger than fiction, it was during those few minutes in time that a paradigm shift occurred, defying all logic, changing our lives forever. But, to quote the famous bard, "The path of true love never did run smooth," and not everyone, particularly Aaron's family, was as happy as we were.

Despite relentless persecution, the two of us clung together, believing the unity we had discovered about our two faiths was worth fighting for. Not even the thousands of miles that eventually separated us could keep us apart.

Finally, the way was opened for us to be married and happiness seemed only days away. But then, in the cruelest twist of fate, I was faced with a choice that would change our lives forever.

PROTECTION OF IDENTITY

A final note about the names used in this book—for his own protection and that of his family, I have not used Aaron's real name or those of any of his family. I have also not identified the rabbis who interviewed me for my conversion or the family that housed me during this time.

PEOPLE OF DIFFERENT FAITHS

To the Jews, Christians, and Muslims who might be reading this book, I ask that you do not judge it until you have read it from beginning to end. There are times when I might appear "anti" one or the other, but I ask you to read on and find out how I really feel about us all. I believe that God loves all people equally, but has different duties for us individually and as nations, and if you read this book in its entirety, you will understand why I say this.

THE PAINTINGS AND PICTURES

As I mention in the book, the paintings were done by me for an exhibition to encourage the Jewish people about the faithfulness of their God and how He keeps every promise. They are in no particular order, but hopefully a feature everyone can enjoy and draw from.

GLOSSARY

At the back of the book is a glossary of all the translations of the Hebrew and Afrikaans words used. When the word is used for the first time, it is in *italics* to encourage you to look up its meaning.

עָבְרוּ עִבְרוּ בַּשְּׁעָרִים "פַּנּוּ דֶּרֶךְ
הָעָם סֹלּוּ סֹלּוּ הַמְסִלָּה סַקְּלוּ מֵאֶבֶן
הָרִימוּ נֵס עַל הָעַמִּים הִנֵּה הֹ הִשְׁמִיעַ
אֶל קְצֵה הָאָרֶץ אִמְרוּ לְבַת צִיּוֹן
הִנֵּה יִשְׁעֵךְ בָּא הִנֵּה שְׂכָרוֹ אִתּוֹ
וּפְעֻלָּתוֹ לְפָנָיו

ONE

I couldn't believe that I was finally here again! As I stepped out of the plane, I stopped for a moment to imbibe the heady Middle Eastern air, dripping with orange blossom and seasoned with dust.

It was 1983 and I all but floated through customs, where the official scrutinized my papers, and then, almost reluctantly, stamped my South African passport, and said, "Welcome to Israel."

I thought, "Welcome home," you mean, but knew better than to say it.

Being an exuberant twenty-three-year-old who had just completed a three-year Graphic Design course in Cape Town, South Africa, travel had always been my passion. After eight months of "doing" England, Europe, parts of America and the Middle East, tiny and dusty Israel had become my favorite; hence my return. It seemed as if God had created an Israeli in spirit in me and I was destined to become "Jewish," with a husband, ten kids and living in Jerusalem! This awesome place, its lifestyle, and its diverse people seemed to be all mine, and the fact that I was not born Jewish made no

1

difference to the deep affection I felt inside. I learned later that for most Zionists, Jews and Christians, the City of Jerusalem becomes home to you and a strange occurrence happens in your heart, telling you that you'll return, and here I was!

I had never been to a place before, or since, where the physical and the spiritual worlds connected so meaningfully, and at times merged.

Israel, back then, was a haven for youngsters like myself, where the kibbutz volunteer system met our every need. They supplied the accommodations, outstanding food, and loads of opportunities to meet wonderful people and have ourselves a complete ball. In return, we supplied the labor that kept the kibbutz going. At "twenty something," waking up at 4 a.m. to pick fruit was just another wonderful experience. Oh, how things have changed!

More importantly for me, though, was the time I had to soak up the lifestyle and mind-set of the local Israelis. I was awed by how committed the people were to eke life out of the wilderness, and marveled at how anything could grow at all. Out of seemingly lifeless ground came cucumbers, melons, tomatoes, and countless other riches. I noticed, too, the joy in simple things, like just "being together" as a family or a group of friends. Life itself was precious and the time God had given to each and every one of them was truly enjoyed to the utmost.

I also noticed their readiness to deal with war if terror raised its ugly head again. The fact that every young male and female Israeli school-leaver was put into an army uniform and made to carry a gun, and then again well into his or her adult life, was just part of this unusual place. Fortunately, at that time, there was peace in and on the borders of Israel, and life for both Jew and Arab carried on fairly normally.

Reveling in life in the shadow of death was a bittersweet dichotomy, and something I struggled to understand. Despite, or perhaps *because* of this, it did not take long before I fell in love with this land of contrasts.

Peaceful folk songs around a starry skied campfire to angry shouting between kibbutz members about some or other dispute are both part of this "*Sabra soup!*" Sabra is the name given to a Jewish person born in Israel, meaning "prickly pear"—tough and prickly on the outside, but soft and sweet on the inside; and this they are!

It was during the third month of my life on Kibbutz *Revivim* that I received a phone call from a good friend, Bev Huch, an Australian who worked for the International Christian Embassy of Jerusalem. Bev was the Personal Assistant to the director and they were looking for an artist to help them out for the up-and-coming Feast of Tabernacles. Knowing my artistic abilities and that I was in the country, she suggested to her boss that they invite me to help, not realizing for one moment the impact this would have on my life.

The bags under my eyes testified that I was now getting a little tired of the early mornings and the late night discos, and I gleefully accepted the invitation, thinking that a quieter life in Jerusalem would do me some good. Then, of course, there was that thirst that had never gone away, and I knew that finally living there, after just dreaming about it, would pour water on my parched soul.

The bus trip from the Kibbutz to Jerusalem was a see-sawing of emotion as I did not know what lay ahead of me after the secure three months on the Kibbutz. And then, before I knew it, I was there, passing by the "old city" with its sandstone walls and maze-like streets. It was dusk and the buildings seemed loathe to relinquish the sunlight they had absorbed during the day. The yellow pinkish hue of the walls created a watercolor impression, breathtaking to my artist's eye. It was then that I knew that my thirst for Jerusalem would never be quenched.

At this moment, as the sun set over the city, there was no thought of flying back to South Africa. I was already home. A brand new chapter in my life had begun and I knew there was no turning back.

TWO

I had been working for the Christian Embassy now for a few months. It was Jerusalem, 1984, and once again The Feast of Tabernacles was about to be celebrated. The Feast is one of the seven major festivals that God has commanded the Jewish people to keep. It is celebrated over seven days, commemorating the time when God Himself protected and provided for the people of Israel in the wilderness. Even though they lived in vulnerable booths or shelters in this hostile environment, they survived, and so to commemorate this, the people of Israel construct small shelters and have their meals in them to remember God's protection and His promise to *tabernacle* and dwell amongst them again one day.

Having spent some time in the Negev, I could understand a little of what the people went through during the forty years of wandering. God had miraculously provided for the Israelites back then just as He is still doing in a different way for their descendants on the kibbutzim—bringing forth life where previously there was none.

For the last twenty years the International Christian Embassy of Jerusalem has taken the prophetic step of sending out God's calling to all Christians everywhere to worship Him in Jerusalem during this annual festival. Unlike the other six Jewish festivals that center only on Israel, this one includes the other nations and portrays the time when God, through the Messiah, will come and rule the world in peace and justice, anticipating the Messianic Age.

In the book of Zechariah 14 verse 9 it says: *And the Lord shall be King over all the earth: in that day shall there be One Lord, and His name One.*

In verses 16 - 19 it carries on: *And it shall come to pass, that every one that is left of all nations which came against Jerusalem, shall go up from year to year to worship the King, the Lord of hosts, to keep the feast of Sukkot (Tabernacles). And it shall be that whosoever will not come up of all the families of the earth unto Jerusalem to worship the King, the Lord of hosts, even upon them shall be no rain.*

So at this time each year thousands upon thousands of Christians from across the globe come to Jerusalem in a prophetic act to worship the God of Israel with His people, the Jews, in anticipation of this time to come.

Working on this project was one of the most exciting times of my life. Imagine me, this young, inexperienced artist from South Africa, commissioned to paint 20-metre murals of Jerusalem, as it was 2000 years ago, with the Second Temple in all its splendor!

So electrifying was my life that I felt God to be only a local phone call away! Spiritually and creatively, I began to thrive as never before and my fulfillment was obvious to everyone who saw my work.

Being a dab hand at anything creative (even the odd hair cut for staff members if they were brave or poor enough!), my job description also included designing brochures, costumes, corporate logos, and stage sets.

But one bright, sunny morning, my duties took on a different shape. Rollie, our pretty Indian receptionist, took ill. So, being the general "do-it-all girl," I was called upon to become an instant receptionist.

My ignorance compelled me to accept the position with gusto. I mean, how difficult would answering the odd telephone call be? And surely I could handle preparing tea for any guests who might drift in, all the while keeping a nice cheery smile. Oh, and if I were asked about the history and future of the Embassy—no problem, this was one of my hobbyhorses.

After the first day I knew I was in serious trouble! Nobody had told me about the "Elijahs" and "Messiahs" who would waft in, proclaiming their divinity. It seems that a place like Jerusalem, the Holy City of God, attracts all kinds of weird and wonderful wackos! As I soon discovered, emotionally unstable people arrive from all over the world, sincerely hoping to fulfill their spiritual fantasies here.

Thank goodness for Ord Derby, a British gentleman and fellow staff member. This particular morning, with monocle neatly tucked under his bushy left eyebrow, he was searching furiously for something in a drawer next to me, when in burst a "messiah!" With an outstretched hand, the "messiah" warmly greeted both of us with a pious, "Shalom, Brethren."

Thankfully Ord's many years of experience living in Jerusalem came to the fore as I just stood by speechless. Quick as a flash, Ord, monocle popping from his eye, took the man's hand and shook it firmly, answering in pucker Queen's English: "O, Shalom to you, too, old boy, do take a seat and I will be with you in a seccie!" and continued scratching in the drawer. The unacknowledged and visibly (in more ways than one) shaken "messiah" promptly did an about-turn, and wafted out the door, never to be seen again.

The following day I was advised to prepare for two dignitaries from the Israeli Government who had accepted an invitation to visit the Embassy and receive a gift. The Director of the Christian Embassy was to present them with a bronze sculpture of Golda Meir, one of Israel's former prime ministers, and the only woman.

Having just learned the basics of the Hebrew language, I was very keen to put it to good use. So, while preparing the tea, and with some impressive sentences in my mind, I was totally unaware of their arrival. Suddenly turning around, armed with a tray-full of tea things, I bashed right into one of them, knocking everything everywhere.

I heard myself saying "Oh, *slicha*, you must be the gentlemen who have come to see Golda's bust!"

One of the men, with a very amused look on his face, smiled and said politely, "Well, I suppose you *could* say that!"

Unfortunately, my boss heard and saw it all. My days at this specialized job were numbered, but I had gained an enormous respect for the receptionists of this world. Seeing them do their jobs with such grace and skill had misled me into believing that it could be done by anyone, even an over-enthusiastic artist!

Although my career in corporate reception wasn't going anywhere, I have these few hours to thank for an unexpected turn that was to change my life forever.

It was a Friday with only two more hours to go before I retired as a receptionist for good. It was the glorious start of Shabbat, and the usual magical anticipation filled the air. A unique peace seemed to pervade everything in Jerusalem as preparations were being made for this weekly Queen of Festivals.

While I was praying for a peaceful last hour or so, an angry young Jewish man burst into the office. My heart sank and if there had been a panic button around, I would have used it. His expression told me that he was not there to make friends, in spite of which I politely asked if I could assist him in any way.

"Yes, you can," he snapped, "by leaving us Jews alone, and getting out of our country!"

A surge of indignation rushed through me and I was struck dumb for a good few moments—which is unusual for me. When my temper subsided I realized that I understood why he was so angry, and didn't blame him for his outburst.

Composing myself, I asked for a few minutes of his time to try and explain what we were doing in his country. He didn't answer me and refused my invitation to sit. Fortunately I knew better than to offer him any refreshments, as was the custom, because with his being Kosher, as other observant Jews, he could not accept food or drink from a non-Jew.

Still standing, he told me he was on a private mission to see "this place," which was an abomination in his country and must be closed down.

I looked around desperately to see if there was anyone else who could help me, but it was clear that I would have to handle this one on my own. As calmly as possible I asked him if he minded telling me how he had come to hear about the Embassy, and what knowledge he had of "true" Christianity, at which he snapped, "Why should I, and what do you care, anyway?"

This was my opportunity. I hurriedly launched into an explanation about how much we really did care, and why exactly we were there. He listened restlessly, but I knew I had his full attention when I mentioned our remorse and deep sorrow about the atrocities committed in the name of Christianity in the past.

"Even until today," I told him, "the Church's doctrines and traditions have drifted so far from their origins, that it appears to be a separate religion and an enemy of the Jews. We, at the Embassy, are a body of

Christian people, representing enlightened believers from around the world who want to say that we are desperately sorry, and wish to do something practical to help repair this huge and tragic rift caused over the centuries.

"One of the many ways we hope to reconcile Jews and Christians is by fulfilling the Scriptures, where the Gentile nations are invited to come and celebrate the feast of the Tabernacles with the Jews in Jerusalem, which is prophetic of the Messianic age to come."

I also mentioned our belief that the Word of God assured the Israelis' right to their land, being their inheritance forever, given to them by God Himself. This is the very reason we call ourselves Christian Zionists: not merely to come and be in the land where our Lord walked, but to assist the Jews to defend what is rightfully theirs, and to show our solidarity despite world opposition. We believe that if God had abandoned His promises to the Jewish people's forefathers, then the entire Christian faith would be invalid.

We also produced a vast amount of information, I told him, posted out into the Christian world, informing people of the false teachings and perceptions the Church has had of Israel, such as the belief that the Church has replaced Israel.

God's divine purpose for His people, the Jews, and the land of Israel still stands, making it the pivotal point around which God has promised worldwide redemption and future everlasting peace.

It was our task, I said, to remind the Jews of their God-given task to be a blessing to the nations and to encourage them in this tough process. The fact that thousands upon thousands of Jews were returning to the land was not a political accident, but a direct fulfillment of the prophecy that said that this would be one of the signs before the coming of their Messiah.

I tried to point out also that we were not a missionary organization, but members of a body of Christians representing many others, who wanted to play a part financially and prayerfully in restoring Zion and its people to their land. Whew! I was done!

By the shocked look on his face, I knew that he had had a cataclysmic mind-shift. By grace and grace alone, little I, with a huge dose of God's help, had done it! My genuine conviction and heart's cry had been clearly heard and received, and I felt as relieved as I would imagine a mother feels after giving birth. In spite of this young man's initial animosity, I realized that I had brought some light to his murky understanding.

My impassioned oratory had brought beads of sweat to my forehead and I pushed back a long auburn tendril that had forced its way out of the leather thong unsuccessfully trying to keep the rest of my mop at bay.

What an unholy vision I must have been preaching to him—in his conservative Orthodox clothes—about God's plan for the nations, while wearing my favorite Bedouin dress and dangle-dangle earrings that I'd haggled over in Jerusalem's "old market." Oi vei!

Suffice it to say, he was not totally convinced. It sounded all too good to be true, he said, but it was clear that he had not bargained on having such a discussion, and was trying to come to terms with what he had just heard. Not knowing what else to do, he adopted his familiar angry expression.

Once again fully composed, with a disapproving look on his handsome face, he turned on his heel and walked out of the office. But before crossing the threshold he turned quickly and said, "Would you mind if I come back next Friday and we can continue our talk?"

Gripping the desk, I said breathily, "Sure! What's your name?"

"Aaron," he said softly, then less hesitantly, "My name's Aaron." Then he left.

THREE

In Israel there are many different types of Jewish men. There are the ones that smell of garlic and have a Time cigarette dangling from one corner of the mouth and flattery dripping from the other. You find them on street corners during the day and discotheques at night. Don't get too close or you could get more than you bargained for!

Then there are the young soldiers in army uniform, unexpectedly casual to the point of being scruffy—but ever so sexy. Chest hairs sprout from low-buttoned khaki shirts, while pants—always a size too small—are paraded on their journey home for a weekend pass. Youthful pride and physical perfection: a delight to look at for any foreign maiden!

Then there are the older types: less conspicuous but just as smooth. Posed for play, in more ways than one, they sit outside coffee shops matching their wits over board games. Even with checkmate only a few moves away, they never miss the chance to flash a wink or blow a kiss at a passing damsel before overpowering their opponent. Ladies, scurry past, or you could be their next conquest!

What is it with these Israeli men? Sex appeal and confidence ooze from every pore, making every woman feel flattered and adored. Let's face it, most Israeli men are good looking and they know it. Having perfected the art of boosting the ego of any woman—no matter what shape or size—with their declarations of "love," it's Paradise for most gullible, egocentric, western women. And let's face it, ladies, most of us are.

But Aaron wasn't like any of them. Just as he'd promised, he came back the next Friday, and the next, and we continued our debates. I discovered that he was serious, highly intelligent, superbly skilled, and very religious.

He was the total opposite of any of the other Israeli men I'd met. He was obnoxious, arrogant and aloof, and in a way I found it quite refreshing. But there was no way a matchmaker, Jewish or otherwise, would put the two of us together. My tasselled pants, hippy shirts, eccentric scarves, and "Jesus" sandals were, to him, an Orthodox Jew, exactly what a nice marriageable girl *shouldn't* wear. But he didn't seem to see me most of the time, and rarely, if ever, established eye contact. I knew for certain that it wasn't I he was after on our weekly visits, but what I believed in and had to share with him, so I asked God to give me the words to say.

It was around the fourth visit that I began to feel extremely inadequate and unable to answer his countless questions. I desperately needed to introduce him to other people of similar intellectual and religious caliber. His unbelievable mind and hungry heart overwhelmed me and I could no longer explain why I believed the way I did, or how I could be so pro-Israel without telling him about "Yeshua" (Jesus). This I knew would freak him out and I would probably lose him as a friend for good. So what was I to do?

I knew that it amazed him to think that a girl like me, with no Jewish blood in her veins, could have so much zeal for a people and a land that weren't her own. Why would I leave my home and family to come and show love and support for the Jews, when in many cases I wasn't even trusted or received? Yet I, along with other Christians, continued to press on to fulfill the Scripture to: "*Comfort ye, comfort ye, my people.*" This completely baffled him, and he needed to understand more.

Being very much aware of most Jewish people's aversion to even hearing the name of Yeshua, I tried my utmost not to offend Aaron by tiptoeing through the minefield for as long as I could. Then one day, choosing my words very carefully, I tried to explain that once we are touched by Hashem's *Ruach Hakodesh*, our spiritual eyes are opened and He reveals things to us that which no amount of studying or intelligence can discover. This is when the miracle of salvation takes place, and the truth about God's son Yeshua is planted in our hearts.

Having come thus far, and the waters remaining calm, I continued to tell him that the Spirit gives us a love for the things that He loves, one being Israel and its people.

I had said most of this without looking directly at him, so decided to take a quick peek to see how he was handling it. His face was impassive, even calm. What a relief!

But then he exploded! Seldom have I seen such an outburst of rage as he realized what I had been saying. From that moment on, his one and probably very last Christian friendship was over.

A torrent of accusations came pouring out, calling me a "typical, sly missionary." Then he got up to leave, spitting out his last words: "If "*He*" was the Messiah, don't you think our God would have told us that Himself?" Before I had time to think, I heard myself saying timidly, "But He did!" Then he stormed out the room, so that he wouldn't have to listen to this blasphemy any longer.

Need I say just how helpless and pathetic I felt? I was sure that I would never hear from Aaron again. I knew so little about him—where he lived or what he did for a living—so had no way of contacting him to explain that I intended neither to offend nor convert him, which, I believed, was God's job. It seemed that my blunder had destroyed the opportunity for friendship.

Why was Yeshua such a stumbling block? I realized that nothing had changed for two thousand years; the message of grace proclaimed by Jewish prophets is still disbelieved and is an offense to most Jews. Like many well-meaning Christians before me, I'd blown it.

Days and weeks passed. My heart was crushed, not only because I knew that I had upset him, but because, to my horror, I realized I was actually missing him! I was in serious trouble. Was I in love? How on earth could this be? I knew, oh, so well, that this man was out of bounds, and yet I could not stop thinking about him. What was it about his life that fascinated me so? I even loved his arrogance. "Oh, Lord, help me forget him," I prayed.

They say time heals, but they lied, and I scanned the streets and shops, hoping to catch a glimpse of him again. Then one day, while crossing a busy street, there he was! He saw me too, and turned for a moment as if to pass me by. My heart stopped, then started beating again as he drew me aside and asked how I was doing. "Fine," I answered, not too truthfully. "That's good," he said. But just as I thought that would be the end of our conversation, he started to talk.

I looked at his beautiful face and listened hungrily for words that might suggest he had missed me too. I thought I heard the word, "apologize." Apologize for what? I wondered. And then he wanted to know when next we could meet to continue our discussion. My heart leaped. Thanks to the thunder of my raging heartbeat, I missed what he said next. Now it was my turn to apologize, and he had to repeat almost everything he had just said.

I could hardly believe that God had given our friendship a second chance, and as I waited for him to arrive for our appointed "talk," I half expected him not to turn up. But he did, not once, but twice, and the conversations started again.

The third time we met, the atmosphere between us began to relax and I casually asked if he would like to attend a Messianic service. It was going to make things a whole lot easier for us, I thought, if he experienced for himself this wonderful event, where Jewish and Gentile believers in Messiah worship together as one people. He laughed out loud and said he would rather die than defile himself—body, soul, and spirit—by attending such a place.

"Why not?" I protested. To my mind there was nothing wrong with going into other places of worship out of interest or respect for a person of a different faith. I told him that I felt it could only bring more understanding and assurance into my own heart that what I believe in is true. Nothing threatens me anymore, so why should it him?

I told him that Messianic congregations comprise both Jewish and non-Jewish believers in Messiah, although the format of the service is Jewish in style.

It's a fellowship where Jewish believers in Yeshuah can maintain their Jewish identity and feel at home when worshipping God, while Gentile believers feel like they have gone back to the origin of their faith. The Bible says that in the Last Days, Jew and Gentile will be one in Messiah, and these services are a foretaste of the incredible wonder to come.

However, it's not like a religious service in a synagogue where the liturgy is followed, but Jewish believers are free to wear their prayer shawls and pray and praise in a Jewish way. Also, all the Jewish festivals are kept and obeyed, honoring the Word of God in Leviticus 23, where it says that they are God's Holy convocations. Knowing now that Yeshuah did not come to abolish the Law but to fulfill it, the commands become even more of a delight to obey, as He is symbolized in them all.

Aaron's expression was impassive as he absorbed all this new information. As he left that day, I thought that once again I had gone too far.

But two days later he called and sheepishly asked whether my invitation still stood. Well, you could have knocked me over with a feather! He said the following Sunday would suit him, and asked where we could meet, and at what time. Curiosity had finally got the better of this cat!

I waited outside the beautiful oval hall that belonged to the Jerusalem YMCA. Inside the ceilings were decorated with blue and gold art works that I had spent many hours appreciating. I closed my eyes and imagined that I was inside with Aaron at my side. Despite its majestic appearance, the hall had the smell of a mystical, musty cellar where one could imagine treasure might be hidden. The floorboards creaked from pure age and the old wooden seats squeaked. But this was no quiet place of worship and the very foundations of the ancient building were shaken every week.

With the sound of the service warming up behind me, I checked my watch and was pleased to see Aaron arriving at exactly the right time.

"Are you ready?" I asked.

"As ready as I'll ever be," he answered, and followed me into the strange and forbidden place.

I knew he would be uncomfortable attending the service and admired his bravery for doing so, so I hoped to prevent any further embarrassment by purposely arriving late and slipping quietly in the back, hopefully unnoticed by others.

Well, we arrived right in the middle of one of the loudest and liveliest charismatic Hebrew choruses ever written, all about Yeshua being the Messiah of Israel! What had I done? I wanted to flee, but Aaron just stood there. His wide-eyed stare took in the incredible scene, while the congregation was athrob with song and dance.

Jew and Gentile musicians played tambourines and guitars, while others, young and old, male and female, ex-Muslim, Jew and Christian, were reaching a crescendo of clapping, singing, and dancing. Some believers were holding hands and weaving their way around the hall, with the more agile among them skipping and leaping in the air. The more sedate waved their arms in the air and sang with all their might.

I felt like falling through the floorboards, wondering just how long my Orthodox Jewish friend would hold out. With eyes on stalks and shock written all over his pale face, I suggested we leave, but he ignored me. The song ended and I prompted him to sit close to an exit where we could make an escape if necessary, but he brushed me off. He just kept standing there while the service continued. What was he thinking?

Eventually when it was time for the sermon, he came and gingerly sat down next to me. I assured him that he need not stay, but he didn't budge. Why was it that I felt so apologetic when the message of the Messiah should be shouted from the rooftops? Why was I feeling embarrassed when the Bible asks, *"How will they know if they do not hear?"* Then and there I realized that I was scared of losing him, and this was the reason for my dread.

The message that evening could not have been more fitting for the many questions Aaron had, concentrating on all that has been written about Yeshua (which means Salvation) in the Old Covenant and the Prophets. Yet that veil, put there by God Himself, still hangs over the Jewish people's eyes even today. So, like Joseph (a type of Messiah figure) when he became an Egyptian ruler, his very own brothers did not recognize him. Not until later when he ordered his servants out of the room and they were alone, did he take off his Egyptian garb and reveal the real Joseph, their very own brother.

So it will be with the Messiah, Yeshua. He now has a Gentile identity until Father God's set time has come for Messiah, Israel's brother, to come again and lift the veil from their eyes. The veil will remain until the full number of Gentiles comes to salvation through Messiah. The speaker continued: "If the Jews' rejection of Messiah has meant salvation for us Gentiles, what will their acceptance of Him soon be but life from the dead—eternal life!"

This must have been too much for him, because, during the final prayer, Aaron bolted out the back door. I chased after him, bursting into tears as I did so. Aaron's walk was usually fast, but this night I had to run to keep pace with him. A barrage of apologies gushed from my mouth until he could take no more. Suddenly spinning around, he stuck a very angry finger in my face and said venomously, "You people have pinched everything from us! We used to worship God like that! King David also danced before our God!" Then, turning tiredly away, he whispered, "What has happened to us Jews? Why have we lost so much?"

A very angry and confused man climbed onto the bus that night. Without even so much as turning around to wave good-bye, he was gone again!

FOUR

Three months passed without sight or sound of Aaron. My head told me it was best this way, but my heart silently longed for him. I tried to hide the truth about my feelings from my friends—and from myself—but wondered constantly where he was, and what was going on inside his head and heart. I recalled over and over again the conversations and times we had had together, wondering whether any of the growing feelings I felt for him were shared.

Somewhere along the line I had become attracted to more than Aaron's questioning spirit. I remembered the first time I'd noticed the man behind the religious image. That day I was in my little office *cum* studio on top of the Embassy building, when suddenly Aaron appeared in the doorway, silhouetted against the sun. That was the first time he had ever come into "my" space, and immediately the air was charged with something I couldn't put into words. He took my breath away. His shoulders were broad, his legs strong, and his chest, which I could just glimpse through his sun-soaked white shirt, spoke of a physical life beyond his religious studies.

Seemingly unaware of the effect he was having on me, he had lightly stepped into my studio and flopped down on an easy chair. He chatted freely—the first time I had ever seen him so relaxed—and brushed his tousled black hair away from his forehead. I suddenly noticed that his skin was lighter than the average Israeli and his flickering brown eyes, a shade or two lighter than coal. He was still talking, although I can't remember what about, and I noticed his smiling mouth—wide, gentle, and beautiful. His nose, only a little crooked, was finely shaped and had a character all of its own.

I was well aware of the dangers of falling in love with a man like Aaron, but as we sat there, he in an easy chair and me on my desk, I found myself being drawn deeper and deeper into his paralyzing warmth. Then, when he turned his gaze on me, any hope of resistance was gone. It was the first time he had ever really looked at me and I wondered what he saw. We stared at one another for an ageless time, until he asked softly, "Will you join me for Passover?"

I struggled to hold back my tears while trying to get out a simple, "Yes." I was deeply honored that a man so strong, pure, sincere, and spiritually passionate would want to share this special festival with me.

A completely different Aaron came into my life that day. Even his distinctive walk had changed—he could stride into my office with confidence, on a pair of legs worthy of a Michaelangelo sculpture. I shocked him one day by asking if I could see them—the look on his face was priceless! Need I add that I never did see them.

I remembered how he once had laughed at me when I told him about the reality of our enemy, the devil, and how we Christians believed that we must be constantly on our guard against his insidious attacks. His amusement about this strange concept led to a loud outburst of thanks to God for being a "Chosen One," naturally untouched by such bizarre phenomena! I could hardly believe his arrogance, and in true Israeli style, exploded, letting him know how wrong he was, and that one day he might come running to me for help!

By this stage of my time in Israel, I had learned how to stand my ground in a dispute no matter how loud and aggressive the onslaught. To most Israelis, a day is never a good day without an argument or two. Everyone is entitled to his or her opinion, but don't expect anyone to agree with you! Nobody seems to care whether you get offended in the process because "getting offended" is not the issue here—having your say is. This was the way in the Middle East, and I found out fast that if you can't beat 'em, join 'em!

I remembered fondly the one and only argument that Aaron and I had "in public." I still had to learn the art of walking across a busy street with my arm outstretched, fingers pursed and pointing heavenward, which in Israel means a serious *"rak rega!"* I learned from Aaron that when doing this, no matter what is approaching you or at what speed, you just *walk*!

On that particular day Aaron confidently stepped out into rush-hour traffic, while I, being more cautious, hesitated—a *big mistake*, which nearly killed us both!

Surviving the near accident was one thing, but recovering from the aftermath of my "hesitation" was something else! Dragging me out of the path of a rampant truck, Aaron let me, and everyone else within two blocks know that if this skill was not mastered instantly, there was very little hope that I or anyone else crossing with me would live to see another day. Needless to say, I learned the hard way, and from that moment, I became a crossing expert!

Delightful memories teased my mind, making me increasingly lovesick. I had briefly shared a life so rare and different through this man. Was it some kind of sick game to experience something so special only to have it ripped away from me? Why was I so drawn to his Jewish lifestyle? Was love blinding me?

He had probably forgotten my name by now, and here I was, longing for something I would never be a part of. But I was consumed by fantasies of a life with him. Could there be a vague possibility that he was thinking of me, too?

I then decided to turn all thoughts of him into "prayer." Very nice and spiritual, I thought, but what a joke—my prayers just became an excuse to obsess over him even more. Love is blind, so the saying goes, but your neighbors ain't! My dear friends could sense the turmoil inside me, and knew only too well that I was in a very dangerous place. This was not a nice, safe boy in secular America or South Africa, but Israel, Judaism, and Aaron!

Then one morning around 3 a.m. my phone rang, waking me suddenly. Being away from my home country, my mind immediately went wild, jumping to all sorts of conclusions—who had died? When? Where? But no, it was Aaron, and I realized he was in serious trouble.

I barely heard him say, "Pray for me, I can't breathe, it feels as though I am going to die!" His terrified voice scared me stiff and I suddenly became aware of an evil presence all around me. A sulphurous stench flooded my apartment, almost suffocating me to the point where I, too, felt I was going to die. Aaron was having the same experience and I realized that both of us were under demonic attack!

The little knowledge I had gleaned on the subject during my spiritual walk stood me in good stead, and I began to rebuke the evil in the only name that has any authority. Not caring anymore what Aaron would think, I cried, "Jesus! Jesus! Jesus! In Jesus' name, leave us alone!" Immediately, the evil presence and its horrendous stench left both our apartments, and we were safe again.

Neither of us said anything for a while as our hearts stilled and breathing slowed. Before ringing off, he asked if we could meet at six that morning in a small park we both knew of. "Something very serious is happening and I need to talk," he said, then put down the phone.

What was I to make of this? Aaron was back in my life, but there was no wild excitement as I had anticipated. After the extraordinary things we had just experienced, I realized that something awesome must be going on, particularly because I knew his stand on things of *this* nature!

Before that night I had played out many scenes in my head of how I would react if I ever saw him again—what I would say and even what I would be wearing at the time. Childish, I know, but it's how we girls think sometimes.

But there were no fantasies this time—the diabolical encounter had obliterated them. Aaron had called, and he needed my help. What was I going to do? All girlish thoughts disappeared, and as I sat on my bed that night, I matured instantly.

FIVE

It was an autumn morning and the air was crystal clear after the rains, a stark contrast to the stench of the night before. The early morning sun filtered through the trees, softly bathing a lone figure sitting on a bench— it was Aaron, his body crumpled in despair.

Hearing my footsteps, he looked up and I saw my beloved for the first time in months. His face was ashen and visibly changed—his eyes sunken from fatigue, which was also something I had never seen before. My knees went weak.

He didn't greet me, but launched into a babble of incoherent sentences. I tried my best to calm him down. Eventually I understood enough to determine that the attack the night before had come after a mind-blowing revelation. "He's the Messiah. I can't deny it anymore," said Aaron, shaking his head, shoulders slumped. I was shocked rigid.

But Aaron didn't notice the effect his confession of faith had had on me. He continued babbling: "What am I going to tell them? It will destroy them!" I knew he was talking about the unimaginable havoc that would be caused when he told his family. I didn't know what to say to him, and tried to find his hand just to hold it. But it was he who made first contact with his haunted eyes. He was like a child reaching out for a teddy during a storm. I was now his only friend, and he needed me to say something.

I don't remember exactly *what* I said—I was as scared as he was—but he clung to my every word of encouragement and assurance that God would lead the way.

We eventually left the sun-speckled bench, but walked and talked for most of the morning. I could hardly believe what he was telling me.

For this highly intelligent Orthodox Jew to admit that Yeshua is the Messiah is a monumental miracle. Only through divine revelation can a person such as Aaron—or anyone for that matter—ever come to this understanding. I certainly had no intellectual influence— for I was no match for him on this level—but the fact that I, as a Gentile, had such a love for the things of God and Israel had baffled him.

It was during the last three months of silence that he had begun his search—in typical Aaron style—by telling God *not* to bother showing him anything in the *Torah* or the *Tenach* about the Messiah.

He claimed that in these books too many Scriptures get misrepresented and misconstrued, especially by those crazy Christians! Thus God would have to prove that Yeshua *is* or *isn't* the Messiah through the *Talmud*. Only then would he believe.

The Torah consists of the first five books of Moses. The Tenach includes the *Nevi'im* (the books of the prophets) and the *Ketuvim* (the "writings" such as Psalms and Proverbs). The Talmud is a collection of books detailing the normative view of Judaism, written by Jewish sages up until 500 CE (Christian Era).

Totally convinced that he was safe, he began a day and night search for the truth, not expecting to discover anything different from what he already believed and would die for.

But at 2.30 a.m. on "that" morning, he awoke with a sense of restlessness and decided to continue studying. It was then, he said, that the "scales fell from his eyes," as he read and re-read in disbelief a passage in the Talmud about a miracle that happened at the Temple after the death of the certain man.

Not being able to remember too many of these Tulmudic facts, I knew though that it had something to do with atonement.

The age-old veil that has blinded the Lord's people all these years was lifted from his eyes that morning and he could see and understand for the very first time the atoning power of the blood of this Man called, "Salvation!"

This realization was life-changing for Aaron and so much else slotted into place that it made it impossible for him to deny it any longer. It was at that moment that the devil attacked him, trying to terrify him into denying what he had just come to believe.

Immediately remembering my stories of the unseen world—and with his pride now deep in his pocket—he called me in desperation. He said that my prayer for the fear and stench to leave in the Name he only knew before as a swear word had taught him an enormous lesson. He now understood why the devil had to resort to such extreme means.

It's when we fully understand the devil's hatred of the truth that we can grasp why he does the things he does. He is the Father of Lies and loathes to see anyone set free in their understanding of God's way of redemption.

There were obviously a million questions needing answers, but Aaron's biggest concern was, "What does belief in Yeshua make me become?" Was it going to destroy his Jewish identity and all that he had been taught and believed and loved so much? This was his greatest fear. But he had other questions too: "Am I the only Jew to believe this way? How am I going to survive the coming storm? Why does Yeshua have such a Christian identity today, if He is the Jewish Messiah? Does this revelation of Yeshua mean that God is still ONE?" All were still mysteries to him.

In those critical moments, I tried my best to assure Aaron of his unchangeable Jewish heritage, and that to come to faith in the Messiah was the most Jewish thing he could possibly do. It changed *nothing*, except that now he was graciously atoned for by God's own Son. I told him that Jews are called by God to live like Jews, period! But nothing I said seemed to convince or console him.

SIX

Although Aaron and I were back together I felt as if we were sitting on a time bomb. The realization that Yeshua was not just the subject of Christian propaganda, but indeed Israel's promised Messiah, had taken its toll on Aaron's emotional and spiritual well being. He was traumatized and deeply anxious about how his family would react. We Christians call our faith the Good News, but I knew that it would seem anything but good to Aaron's family.

In all Orthodox Jewish families, the first-born son is dedicated as a "first fruit" sacrifice to God, just as the first tenth of all that is earned or produced by any Jew must also be given to Him. The child is expected, more than his siblings, to serve the Lord to the best of his ability by studying Torah and fulfilling his obligations to God. Aaron was the first-born son of the Solomon family.

He was destined to study Torah and live out his calling within his family, the community, and the country. He was now thirty-two and had fulfilled his duty to perfection as a schoolboy, a soldier, a professional engineer, and a religious scholar.

Since birth, Aaron was his parents' pride and joy—physically, mentally, and spiritually blessed by Hashem in abundance. He excelled at whatever he put his hand to, earning the nickname, "Die Wunderkind!" from his family.

At the tender age of four Aaron's exceptional gifts had been recognized. Fun for this young man was to memorize Psalm 119—all 176 verses of it!

His life had always been clearly mapped out and he was fulfilling it to everyone's approval and admiration—until now.

He agonized for days about how he was going to approach his *Abba*—his best friend, his mentor, his hero, his father. Over the years Aaron and his Abba had developed a unique rapport where their common passion for Torah and the things of God bound them together with cords that seemed impossible to break. But now Aaron realized that even this powerful bond was at stake. The love, unity and unquestionable confidence that had been built up between them over the years were now Aaron's only hope. Perhaps his dear father would hear him out and listen to the evidence he had gleaned. Surely his dad would draw on the many years they had been so close, knowing his son to be thoroughly dependable, and grant him a hearing to prove the truth of his discovery.

But these few comforting thoughts didn't dispel the sick feeling he felt as he left me to walk to his parents' apartment that fateful day. Aaron had finally summoned up enough courage to set up an appointment to discuss "something serious" with his Abba. I waited behind, praying as I watched him disappear into the distance. Soon, he was indistinguishable from the other Jewish men as he headed into the Orthodox neighborhood that was so close, yet so far from mine.

His father was waiting in his study, wondering what serious business his son wanted to discuss with him. A promotion at work? Some godly task to undertake through the synagogue? He didn't have to wait long. Aaron quickly greeted his mother in the kitchen with a kiss, then closed the door so the two men could be alone.

He didn't hesitate, having rehearsed what he was going to say for days: "Abba, I've been studying something very important.

"What is it, my son?"

"It's about the One most of the Western world believe is Messiah." Not daring to even say the name.

Mr. Solomon's grey eyebrows came together in a frown, wondering what on earth his special son was doing studying one of the greatest counterfeits in history.

"And what did you discover, Aaron?"

"That it's true. He *is* Messiah. I can't deny it any longer; there's too much evidence." And then, before his father's anticipated eruption, "Please, Abba, let me just *show* you..."

All color drained from his father's face, and he put his hands over his ears and started rocking backward and forwards in his chair. "Lo! Lo! Lo!" he wailed, "No! No! No!"

"But, Aabba, I must tell you why!"

"Lo! Lo! Lo!" Desperately, Aaron tried to reason with him between the wails. "Abba, don't worry, I'm not a Christian now, I'm a 'completed Jew.' Look, the prophet Zechariah spoke of Yeshua as Messiah when he said, '*And I will pour out on the house of David and the inhabitants of Jerusalem a spirit of grace and supplication. They will look on me, the one they have pierced, and they will mourn for me as one mourns for an only child and grieve bitterly for him as one grieves for a first born son.*'"

But the old man refused to listen and carried on grieving for *his* first born son. Refusing to give up, Aaron continued showing him verse after verse from the Tanach and the Tulmud to prove his case, but nothing helped.

Even though every verse backed what Aaron shared, leaving little room for unbelief, the old man chose to close his ears. Then he made the mistake of telling his father about me—his Christian friend!

Mr. Solomon couldn't even look at his son as he said, "You traitor! Get out! Leave this house and don't come back until you have repented and shown yourself faithful to the one true way." Then he started tearing his clothes, the ultimate sign of rejection, signifying that this "person" in front of him is to him as good as dead.

Completely defeated, Aaron turned and left the house, not even stopping to say goodbye to his mother who was weeping in the kitchen.

Unless one has had a similar experience, one cannot begin to comprehend the agony that Aaron was in. I grieved for both him and his family, and found myself weeping uncontrollably for them all. In their minds I was to blame, and I could understand the hatred directed towards me. After all, I was this "evil" person who had poisoned his mind, robbed him of his senses, and disrupted all their lives. Even though this was far from the truth, how were they to know? I knew that if the roles were reversed, it would have been exactly the same for my own family, so I blamed no one.

Poor Aaron was devastated at being cut off from all he had ever known and loved so much. He was now a marked man in his community and considered "dangerous!" There was nothing I could do except be there for him, even though I seemed to be the reason for all his problems. But he never saw it that way and couldn't stop reassuring me of my innocence. We clung to each other, not knowing when the storm was going to end.

I thought that nothing could be worse than what Aaron had already endured, but I was wrong. On the following Shabbat, Aaron, as was his custom, went to the synagogue where he had always played an active role. No one spoke to him. No one looked at him. No one wanted to even stand beside him. He was totally ignored. Obviously the "bad news" had spread like wildfire. Deciding to play it cool and overlook the hurt, he silently prayed for a future miracle.

After the service he planned to pass his parents' home, hoping to see them and somehow convey that faith in Yeshua made him no less a Jew and that absolutely *nothing* about him had changed. But they closed the door in his face. Crushed and rejected, he stumbled through the streets until he found himself outside my apartment.

Not expecting anyone to visit that Sabbath night, I was at first not aware of the gentle knock at the door. I eventually looked through my peephole and could hardly believe my eyes. It was Aaron, his face contorted with grief as rivers flowed down his cheeks. His clean Shabbat clothes were in disarray and he gripped the doorframe to stop himself from collapsing.

I tried desperately to calm him down and to find out what had happened. Eventually he told me. "I can now imagine," he said, his voice breaking, "what Yeshua went through when he was rejected by His very own people whom He loved so much. And yet, He still chose to die for them on that wretched cross." This reminded Aaron of a passage in the book of the prophet Isaiah, chapter 53, which he recited for me through his bitter tears:

"*He was despised and rejected by men—a man of sorrows and familiar with suffering. Like one from whom men hide their faces, He was despised, and we esteemed him not. Surely He has borne our grief and carried our sorrow; yet we esteemed Him stricken, smitten by God and afflicted.*

"But He was wounded for our transgressions, He was bruised for our iniquities; the chastisement for our peace was upon Him, and by His stripes we are healed. All we like sheep have gone astray; we have turned, every one, to his own way; and the Lord has laid on

Him the iniquity of us all. He was oppressed and he was afflicted, yet He opened not His mouth. He was led as a lamb to the slaughter, He as a sheep before its shearers was silent. He opened not His mouth.

"He was taken from prison and from judgement. And who will declare His generation? For he was cut off from the land of the living. For the transgression of My people he was stricken, and they made His grave with the wicked. But with the rich at His death, He had done no violence, nor was any deceit on His mouth. Yet it pleased the Lord to bruise Him; He has put Him to grief.

"When You make His soul an offering for sin, He shall see His seed, He shall prolong His days, and the pleasure of the Lord shall prosper in His hand. He shall see the labor of His soul, and be satisfied. By His knowledge My righteous Servant (Yeshua) shall justify many for He shall bear their iniquities. "Therefore I will divide Him a portion with the great, and He shall divide the spoil with the strong, because He was numbered with the transgressors, and He bore the sins of many and made intercession for the transgressors."

For Aaron there was now no more doubt as to who the Messiah was.

SEVEN

Weeks passed and Aaron continued to be completely shut out of the life he had once lived and loved so much. The news of Aaron's treachery leaked out to his family and friends, and they too cut him off, so as not to bring the family name into any more disrepute. I truly became his only friend.

But then one day we received a glimmer of hope when he received an invitation from the powerful Rabbinical Court, the Vatican of Judaism, to discuss this diabolical change in belief.

Aaron's father was obviously very worried about the decision his son had made and his supposed "proof" to back it up. Because of Aaron's incredible teaching ability, coupled with his amazing intellect, he was a danger to the Jewish community. In desperation, the old man went to the Rabbinical Court for advice.

The Court was the seat of Jewish authority where important issues pertaining to the Jewish way were debated and binding decisions to protect and preserve the Jewish lifestyle were made. They were only too willing to come to Mr. Solomon's aid. The fact that his son had earned such great respect and approval in the past made his conversion a matter of immense importance, so no more time could be wasted.

It was obvious in their minds that nobody of Aaron's caliber would ever succumb to such deception unless vicious missionary tactics had been used to trick him. The fact that he was involved with me, a young Christian woman, confirmed their belief that Aaron had been ensnared. To them I was like the wicked woman of Solomon's proverbs against whom young men are warned: *"My sons, listen to me; pay attention to what I say. Do not let your heart turn to her ways or stray into her paths. Many are the victims she has brought down; her slain are a mighty throng."*

This sort of thing was to be expected among the uneducated, non-religious types, who had always been a soft target for "missionary activities," but not for a man like Aaron. So they agreed to meet with Aaron to hopefully convince him to turn back from the path of idolatry. Aaron was thankful that he would finally have an opportunity to present his case to the top minds in Judaism, but daunted, too. If for all these centuries the rabbis had resisted the truth about Yeshua, then what was it going to take for them to see it now? We prayed that God would direct his words and give him courage and great boldness. Aaron was early for his appointment, but he didn't have to wait long, and he was soon ushered into the inner chamber where the cream of Judaism sat around a large oval table. He saw his father sitting in a leather armchair overarched by hundreds of books containing the very essence of Judaism.

Aaron tried to greet him, but the old man turned away with tears in his eyes. There was nothing more this father could say, and he just prayed that the great men of the Rabbinical Court could succeed where he had failed. It was obvious that all the years of teaching, coaching, encouragement, and investment in his first-born son's life had come to nothing, and unless the rabbis could convince him to repent, Aaron would no longer be his son. So, like a little bird, the old man sat rigid, his panic-filled eyes frozen in fear.

No one around the table greeted him either. There was no need for introductions and they all knew why they were here: to save a Jewish soul.

Brushing aside the usual formalities Aaron was given the floor and asked to explain the reasons for his insane decision. With a deep breath, and a quick but sincere prayer to Hashem, Aaron presented his case in a logical, academically sound manner. Like Peter as he stood before the Sanhedrin in the New Covenant account of the early church, he told them exactly how he had come to believe that Yeshua was the Messiah.

They had dozens of questions, trying to catch him out on the most obscure elements of theology, but he had an answer for everything. Every accusation he refuted, every protestation he tore down. He spoke the truth, and for that there is no answer.

As it had been with his dad, his super intelligence and ability to teach scared them to death. What he said, if true, was too revolutionary to believe.

Suddenly the chief rabbi stood up and declared that the meeting was over. He called his colleagues to vote and their decision was unanimous: Aaron was sworn to secrecy and forbidden to ever talk or mention the name of Yeshua again. If he did, he would be excommunicated.

He was then told to leave immediately. On the way out, no one, including his father, had the courage to look him in the eye.

When Aaron told me about the outcome, he said that he was astounded at the panic surrounding a Jewish man believing in Yeshua when no real fuss is made when Buddha or Hare Krishna are embraced, or, worse still, when someone Jewish believes in nothing! This truly convinced Aaron of the stumbling stone Yeshua said He would be to His people, and also what the Prophet Isaiah had prophesied hundreds of years before, in Isaiah 8 verses 14-16:

"But for both houses of Israel He will be a stone that causes men to stumble and a rock to make them fall. And for the people of Jerusalem He will be a trap and a snare. Many of them will stumble; they will fall and be broken; they will be snared and captured."

But the Rabbinical Council had clearly not given up on Aaron and we were informed that I was now their chief concern. If I was removed, Aaron might be brought back into the fold. My days in Israel were numbered.

EIGHT

Aaron became my strength as the authorities now began their methodical task of ridding the community of my subversive presence. Slowly but surely plans were made to try to keep us apart and, unbeknown to us, look for reasons to deport me.

Threats were made, insisting that we stay apart "or else." But instead of driving us apart, it had the opposite effect—Aaron and I became even more inseparable. Eventually we were being openly followed, twenty-four hours a day. We were watched in the supermarket, movie theater, bank, post office, and any and all public places. Two to three of these "followers'" took turns to dog our every step, and we soon came to recognize them. They even went as far as to follow us to the Messianic fellowship, sitting at the back in utter discomfort, which amused us no end.

Surprisingly they never frightened me, and I even found myself politely greeting them at times!

I even played a little game, imagining I was a celebrity with bodyguards—a fantasy that at least kept a smile on my face during this trying time.

One particular Sunday I had planned to meet Aaron at the evening service. When I arrived I noticed two things: Aaron wasn't there, and my "follower" had two other men with him. Immediately the pastor of our congregation (knowing all about our problems) quickly approached me. He had also noticed the "back-up team," and we both agreed that I should leave before any trouble could erupt in the fellowship. By now most people were aware of our hassles with the authorities, making me feel like I had some kind of dreaded disease.

I ran home that night, looking over my shoulder in case I was being followed, and silently thanked God that Aaron had not arrived. Suddenly I saw a figure beckoning to me from a hiding place among some trees. It was Aaron! Despite the situation, it was rather amusing to see him acting this way because normally he was so bold and brazen.

Aaron had come to the fellowship, but thankfully he was late. He saw the whole scenario unfolding, not quite believing his eyes. The other men with our usual "body guards" were none other than his brothers-in-law from other parts of Israel! They had been urgently summoned by the authorities to come and see for themselves where their beloved brother was going, and with whom! On their part, it was just a "look and see" expedition with no plans to cause trouble.

By this stage my position at the International Christian Embassy had come to an end and I had found myself a gorgeous old stone room in the old city, and had it converted into a delightful art studio for myself.

It was owned by a wonderfully generous Arab-Christian man, and after all the rejection and accusations that had been directed at me, I soaked up his kindness like a sponge.

It was here that George the Arab, Aaron the Jew, and I, the Westerner, caught a glimpse of the Messianic era where only in Yeshua will we be ONE, embodying the unity the world is so longing for.

But George's friendship was rare. As it became increasingly volatile between the authorities and us, our friends diminished rapidly, leaving Aaron and me like a tiny island in a very large and stormy sea.

Then one day, while walking to my little studio in the old city, two men wearing caps grabbed me. They pinned me to a rough stone wall, one of them holding me roughly with his forearm while the other pointed an outraged finger in my face and hissed, "If we see you again with that Solomon boy, we will see your blood flow on these stones!"

Never had I been so threatened and I realized that our persecution had taken a sinister twist for the worse. Naturally, I ran to tell Aaron about what had happened. He was stunned by my story and agreed that we had not until now comprehended the seriousness of our situation.

In Israel there is a group of people called the *Yad La Hachaima*, meaning "The Hand to Life." Their *raison d'être* is to stop the assimilation of Jews to other faiths, seeing it as their duty to save Jewish souls from being "lost." In particular they see the secular and non-religious Jews as a target for "missionaries." The measures taken to save these imperilled souls differed from case to case, depending on the seriousness of the "threat." Our case was obviously considered very serious.

The irony is that the rest of Israel couldn't care less who believes what, or how they go about it, but for the people of the *Yad La Hachaim*, it is a very serious matter.

If I were an Orthodox Jew, I would possibly also support their cause because, after all, Orthodox Judaism is slowly being eroded by secularism, humanism, and every other "ism" there is. So Aaron, as the cream of the Jewish crop, had to be saved at all costs.

One night he arrived unexpectedly at my apartment with a Hebrew newspaper in his hand. He could not hide the amusement on his face as he began to translate an article which was at least half a page long, and all about "me." Although shocked, I also saw the funny side. We did not know whether to laugh or cry at the detail they went into describing me and who they thought I was.

The article was also an exposé of the "organization" I allegedly belonged to that was supposedly made up of women just like me. All young and single Israeli men were warned to watch out for these highly trained "missionary" girls who came from as far away as Australia and South Africa to fulfill their mission. The article claimed that young women were chosen who looked "very Jewish," and were educated in the Jewish culture and language. Their sole purpose in life is to convert just one Jewish man to Christianity and marry him, so to confirm and secure their passport to heaven. These women, according to the paper, called themselves "The Brides of Israel," and were very dangerous, and should be reported immediately if suspected. As bizarre as it sounds, they clearly believed this.

After all, the Jewish Nation has to contend with fundamentalist Muslims who firmly believe that they go straight to paradise if they strap bombs to themselves and die in a holy war against their enemies, the Jews. To a Jewish mind, why would these crazy Christians be any different?

Nothing more was needed to tell us that I was now firmly on their hit list. To them, this particular "bride" must have an unbelievable spiritual, mental, and emotional arsenal to have ensnared a man like Aaron! I started to panic, worrying about our lives and our time together, but not Aaron! For him, it had just begun, and he was looking forward to the fight!

ויכנעו עמי אשר נקרא שמי עליהם ויתפלל
ויבקשו פני וישבו מדרכיהם הרעים ואני אשמע מן השמים
ואסלח לחטאתם וארפא את ארצם

*T*his movie-like cloak and dagger lifestyle was not the only thing going on in our lives, and, ironically enough, this was one of the happiest times in my life. I loved the Jewish lifestyle that I was becoming increasingly involved in, and of course, Aaron was an important part of my life, too. I thank God that so much love and friendship enveloped me during that time or else I would never have survived.

We could deal with the persecution from the authorities, but persecution from Aaron's family was something that continued to hurt him (and me) deeply. We prayed about it daily, asking Hashem to intervene and bring about reconciliation. He answered our prayers.

One of Aaron's sisters and her husband decided that they wanted to meet the woman who had turned their brother's life upside down.

We planned to meet at the King David hotel for supper. I was a bundle of nerves, particularly because I had a partially paralyzed face, brought on by stress. Three days prior our meeting, I awoke and discovered that the left side of my face was completely numb, making eating difficult and drinking impossible. You can imagine how unattractive it looked and how unbelievably embarrassed I was.

A flying visit to the doctor revealed that due to fear and shock, my facial muscle had collapsed. I was ordered to stay indoors out of the cold, and try to remain calm! I also noticed that the hair on the sides of my head had gone grey! Being only twenty-six years old, I was horrified and wondered what else would happen if the stress continued. The doctor was worried and so was I until after two weeks I could see and feel an improvement.

But first I had to get the meeting with Aaron's family out of the way.

It was the beginning of winter and the rains had begun. As we approached the imposing five star hotel, brollies in hand and our collars turned up to the cold, my heart was beating ten-to-the-dozen.

Aaron's sister looked like she might be the first in his family to face up to the fact that I was in her brother's life whether they liked it or not—so I obviously wanted to make a good impression.

As we ran in out of the rain, and the porters whisked away our wet coats and umbrellas, I was left wearing my most conservative dress and stockings—which I rarely, if ever, wore. My wild red hair was tamed into a demure bun, leaving a few wisps for softness.

"You look perfect," Aaron reassured me, squeezing my hand. He obviously wasn't talking about my paralyzed face that made me look like a stroke victim and, of its own will, twitched embarrassingly! But I squeezed his hand back, prayed that my face would behave, and then braced myself to meet the intimidating couple.

We were ushered out of the plush foyer into the regal lounge where Aaron's sister Yael and her husband Moshe were waiting for us.

The carpet was so soft that I felt that I was floating, which did nothing to help my need for reality.

Even though I was heading towards a meeting that could change Aaron's and my life together significantly, I felt like I was in a dream—particularly when I looked out of the massive picture window.

It was my Jerusalem engulfed in a low, misty cloud that swirled about the ancient walls glowing from the powerful floodlights. It was a golden mist under a black velvet sky, bathing the Jaffa Gate and the city's palms in its gentle embrace.

"It's going to be all right," my beautiful Jerusalem whispered, bringing tears to my eyes.

"It's going to be all right," echoed Aaron, pulling me back down to earth as we approached the seated couple. Yael, his sister, saw my reaction to the view and was touched, I think, to see how much I obviously loved the city.

"She's beautiful, isn't she?" said Yael. "Yes, she is, " I said sincerely.

Then came the formal introductions.

Yael, Aaron's sister, was a conservatively dressed Jewish woman in her early forties. Her expression was serious, but not unkind.

Her husband, Moshe, in complete contrast to his wife, was a large, loud, boisterous, New York Jew— the son of a butcher—who put me at ease immediately with his laughing mouth and smiling eyes. He spent most of the evening trying to rescue his *kippa* that kept slipping off his balding head. He became an instant friend and I never once sensed him judging me.

Early on in the evening he whispered in my ear that he could not wait for me to join the family and assured me that everyone else would soon feel the same.

He said that there had been a huge uproar when he wanted to marry Yael, even though he was a Jew, because his father owned a *"pork"* butchery in Manhattan.

"If they could get over that one, they can certainly get over you," he laughed.

Yael, on the other hand, was doing her duty in questioning me about why I had come to Israel and what I wanted to achieve by living in a land for Jews. It was wonderful how all my answers flowed, skew face and all.

Aaron, as usual, just let me be me as I prattled on, periodically squeezing my knee under the table to assure me I was "doing great." In among the millions of questions, the meal, as expected, was delicious, and we all decided to take a look at the dessert menu to round things off.

I had eaten some very tender veal and now, with my new found confidence, proudly announced that I thought cheesecake sounded perfect! One jabbing look from Aaron told me I had said something very wrong and suddenly I remembered that according to Jewish law, one can't mix milk and meat! Oops! Blushing for my sake, Moshe lent over and joked that it had also taken him a long time to get used to all this Kosher business. But since marrying Yael, and becoming religious, he had slowly but surely learned all the ins and outs of Jewish living, so I, too, was not to worry. He was a gem of a man and it was an evening never to forget.

Once Yael gave her apparently positive report back to the Solomon family, things slowly began to soften towards Aaron. His Abba could obviously no longer stand his son's absence, and he began to trust that Aaron would keep his promise to keep quiet about Yeshua. So, much to Aaron's delight, he was invited to join his father once again for their usual debates and discussions and was welcome to sit down with the rest of his family for meals. Aaron felt like the prodigal son, once lost but now found, and the joy of being part of his family welled up in him once more.

But the authorities were not so forgiving. Aaron had been previously married—most unusual for an Orthodox Jew as religious as he was. In a case like Aaron's, despite great unhappiness and incompatibility, the couple together with the community would do everything in their power to save the marriage, especially if they had children. Sadly, in this case, the marriage couldn't be saved, but Aaron still saw his children regularly, and took his responsibility as their loving father very seriously.

The authorities decided to use this against him and threatened never to allow his children to see him if he broke the "rules." Out of pure fear of losing his little ones, Aaron played the game to perfection, not daring to even breathe or whisper the unmentionable name ever again. God would have to understand for now.

Gradually the dust began to settle, but nevertheless a close watch was still kept on us in the hope that I would eventually just go away.

But at least Aaron's family had warmed to him. Wonderfully, his dad took him back completely, and the cutting words, "You are not our son and you have no children," were not repeated.

Things were not that easy for me. Even after his sister and her husband's positive report, I was still a far cry from what they had planned for their special son's life—and I knew it.

With this new persecution complex, I wanted to slink around back alleys and keep out of the public eye—but not Aaron! He would book tickets for the theater and proudly walk me through the crowds, refusing to succumb to the "shame" of being in love with me. Even so, I couldn't come to terms with being the cause of so much pain. One half of me wanted to flee, regardless of my deep love for Aaron, while the other half couldn't bear to be wrenched away from the incredible Jewish lifestyle that was filling a void in my life. All I ever wanted was to be a blessing, not a curse, but with so many lies and misunderstandings about me, there seemed no hope. Only God could work this one out.

However, Aaron remained full of faith, constantly teaching and loving me through it all. Often he would say that in time, once his family got to know me, they would love me as everyone else did and that I would be the light he had always longed for in his family. I tried desperately to remind him that this was tradition, the Rabbinical Court, and religious fury. He retorted, "But Liz, we need people like you in Israel. They just don't know it now, but in time they will. You wait and see!" Aaron was a born fighter who never gave up.

He was also a superb teacher, and continued to coach me in the Jewish way, a richness and fullness so divine that it seemed as if it was meant to be part of me. Why was it that I did not feel like a stranger here despite the persecution? Why did it all seem so right and fitting?

I began to understand that this way was probably very similar to the way Yeshua Himself lived while here on earth. So where had Christianity parted ways with Judaism and become a vastly alien and completely different "religion"? The fact that all the separate original believers in Messiah were Jewish and remained Jewish in culture and lifestyle until their dying days, raised some questions in my mind.

Sadly, I realized that our very precious Jewish roots had been abandoned along the way and exchanged over time for pagan traditions. This had put a wedge between

Jewish and Gentile believers seemingly forever. However, I wanted my roots back and defied anyone to keep me from achieving this!

I set myself to the task with relish, discovering piece by piece how Judaism and Yeshua fit together like a hand in a glove, the one not making sense without the other. Christianity and Judaism have independently strived for self-fulfillment unsuccessfully. The result is a Christian Church not recognizing its Jewish roots and its duty to love them and not boast over them, and the Jews, not playing their role in being a light and example to other nations.

I felt that I had "come home" after a long, frustrating journey of unanswered questions. In spite of all the pain and misunderstanding, it was wonderful that God would eventually fulfill His Word and make the two one.

TEN

One night I couldn't sleep. I lay awake with millions of thoughts racing through my head. I was thinking about all I had learned over the past months about the Jewish way and how it fit so perfectly with my Christian faith. But they weren't peaceful thoughts—I was so anxious, in fact, that I thought I was going to have a panic attack. Could I be going mad?

What was wrong with me? Why was my mind in such turmoil? And then, with crystal clarity, a thought came to mind: "Elizabeth, you must convert!" Convert to what? I was already converted, so what was going on?

Slowly the anxious thoughts were replaced by a rising excitement as I began to grasp what it would mean to become Jewish. I would become like Ruth in the Bible—Aaron's people would become my people, and Aaron's God, my God! But He was already my God! Was I going crazy to think, even for one second, that this could be God's voice? No, it had to be my own madness, and this was dangerous stuff.

I didn't make any decisions that night, it was far too big a step to take on only two hours' sleep. But I couldn't put it out of my mind and I knew I had to talk to someone about it soon.

The following day when I told Aaron about my crazy night, cracking a few jokes to lighten the situation, he went pale, and silently thanked God for this long-awaited moment.

But instead of saying anything, he simply reached out and drew me to him. He held me for a moment and I could feel his heart beating against my chest. Then he took his hand and ran his fingers through my hair, brushing my neck with his knuckles as he did so. I inhaled sharply, feeling sensations that I had never felt with Aaron before. He felt it, too, and pulled back from me slightly, looking at my face. Then, still wordless, he closed his eyes and kissed me while allowing his strong hands to trace the line of my back. I felt as if my entire being was wrapped up in that moment and I didn't want it to end.

Now, as unbelievable as this may sound in our day and age, up until this point in our relationship Aaron and I had had very little, if any, 'romantic contact' other than the natural touches of friendship and comfort. After I shared my experience of the night before with him, he touched me romantically for the very first time. It was this electrifying moment that made us believe that we would be one forever. In that instant, our worlds merged and I knew, without a doubt, that I wanted to become Jewish.

Aaron had been waiting, wisely knowing that until I had had this extraordinary shift in heart, there would be little hope for us as a couple and to still live in Israel. His patience, together with unbelievable respect and love for me, showed I had found a man who had fallen in love with my spirit and soul before my body, the way it was intended by God from the start. We were in *real* love!

With this new turn of events and the powerful shift in our relationship, a bond was formed that washed away my every doubt and fear about becoming his wife. The paralyzing fear that had racked my body and mind were gone, and it seemed like I could take on the whole world.

I will never forget the day Aaron showed me around his apartment for the first time. In the past, with all the difficulties and harassment it had been out of the question for me to visit his home.

He showed me his kitchen, his lounge, his study, then his bedroom. I couldn't believe what I was seeing. There, before my eyes was a "sheet," the kind that extremely religious ultra Orthodox Jews use! You know, the kind you see in movies or read about in books—the one where a man lies on one side and the woman on the other—the one with a hole in it! My expression must have said it all, because Aaron quickly assured me that it was an old sheet his mom had, and she had made a sort of duvet out of it for him after his divorce. Still not quite convinced, I fished to make quite sure that his "sect" of Judaism really did not use sheets like that. He laughed out loud, but caught himself midway, suddenly becoming very shy and embarrassed.

Now, both of us were embarrassed. But I discovered that Aaron's discomfort was not about the sheet or about sex, as I had thought, but about another side of his life.

Aaron had always been a scholar, and having an IQ way above average, studing was his life—and he loved it. Torah was in itself a joy far beyond everything else, so he was content and felt that he lacked nothing in his complete, Jewish life. It was only when he laughed out loud about the sheet that he realized he had never heard himself laugh so loudly before. It sounded odd and it embarrassed him.

Thankfully laughter became a common sound in our lives after that, and his mother re-nicknamed him, "Die Kind," saying that all "Die Wunder" part of him had gone!

One bright, crisp morning Aaron unexpectedly bounced into my apartment and invited me to accompany him to a friend's jewelry shop to purchase an engagement ring! Too choked with emotion to even say, "Yes," we set off together to buy the ring.

He took me to a typical little run-down shop, with a dizzying selection of merchandise. Aaron and I stood closely, discussing the pros and cons of each ring, much to the shock of the very religious assistants.

You must not forget that, particularly in Jerusalem, people are identified by their dress. Aaron was obviously Orthodox, but me? I still dressed the way I always had: arty outfits that were outlandish to an Orthodox eye. Aaron never said a thing about the way I dressed as he saw the inner me. So who cared? Obviously the assistants did, and made no bones about it. Their faces said it all:

"What is this nice Orthodox boy doing with this *Shiksah*?" However, in spite of the inquisitive looks and my embarrassment, we finally walked out of there with a ring on my finger and overflowing with utter joy.

Little did I realize what this would mean to my dear parents back in South Africa. They were devastated to hear about our engagement: "Why can't Elizabeth's life be normal and straightforward, as our other daughters? Going to the Middle East was bad enough, but now this! Our special baby girl in love with a Jew, and a fanatic, by the sound of things! He has to be the one responsible for having poisoned her sweet Christian mind into converting!"

How was I going to explain, and how could I expect them to understand? As difficult as it was for Aaron to try to show his parents and family the "Jewishness" of Jesus, I now had to try and show my parents the "Jewishness" of Christianity. *Oi vey*—what a task!

His parents had gradually grown used to the idea that I was in their son's life, but for them, it was not forever—just a bit more time, they thought, and it would all fizzle out.

Their previous tactics to keep us apart had had the reverse effect, so turning the heat off and playing it cool seemed the next best thing to do. And they hadn't even seen me yet. But now unbeknown to them, I was engaged to their son, and I knew that sooner or later we would have to meet!

ELEVEN

One evening I was on the way to Bible study and decided to walk past Aaron's apartment, hoping to sneak a quick visit. As I rounded the corner, I saw, much to my delight, his lights on. I knocked and quickly hid behind a nearby wall to playfully spring a surprise on him. But before I realized what was happening, Aaron was out in a flash, grabbing me in an army type grip, and covering my mouth. While I was marveling at his agility and war-like skills, as well as enjoying his warm body next to mine, he whispered gently in my ear, "My love, my parents are inside, so it's now or never!"

My heart nearly leaped right out of my chest at the prospect. I was wearing my tight pink jeans that I knew I should never have worn ever again, let alone now! Not forgetting the brown leather boots up to the knees and a baggy bright orange jersey that had seen better days! Added to these horrors was my see-through, bright pink, Bedouin plastic basket with a huge Old and New Covenant Bible inside! I could not have created a worse impression for meeting my hostile future in-laws if I had tried.

"No, Aaron," I protested, "it can't be now, please, not like this!" Aaron held me at arms-length to see what his folks would be faced with. Smilingly he whispered, "Come, my love, you'll be fine. Just be yourself." But that was the problem; I was.

Wanting to run a mile to the nearest orthodox Jewish clothing store, I took a deep breath and said, "OK, it's now or never."

"That's my girl!" said Aaron approvingly.

He gripped me firmly by the hand and half-dragged me over the threshold into what had now become the lion's den.

And there they were—Aaron's much loved, but much feared by me, parents.

Mr. Solomon wore a conservative black suit with a white shirt, even though it wasn't a Friday. His black brimmed hat was on the coffee table and his kippa covered a shock of silver hair. His long grey beard went down to the second button on his shirt, and his moustache covered a quivering upper lip. No doubt he was as scared as I was.

His wife remained rigidly seated, staring ahead, not even acknowledging my presence with the slightest of nods. She wore a maroon, ankle-length dress with thick stockings and lace-up shoes. Other than her face and hands, not an inch of flesh was showing, and I silently thanked God that I wasn't wearing one of my more revealing little numbers—orange and pink were bad enough! On her head she wore a very unfashionable *shattel*—a caricature of an Orthodox Jewish matron.

"*Abba, Emma*, this is Elizabeth,"

"Shalom," said Mr. Solomon, more kindly than I expected. His wife didn't say a word.

You could have cut the atmosphere with a knife as our two worlds tried to gel for the first time. Choosing to ignore the icy response from Mrs. Solomon, I started a tense and rather superficial conversation with Mr. Solomon, to which he politely gave one-word answers. Even though I felt so out of my depth, I prattled on in a performance which, in retrospect, I see was worthy of an Oscar.

In the meantime Aaron appeared totally relaxed, seated comfortably on the couch opposite us, watching the scene unfold. Just one glance at him in this relaxed pose gave me the most unbelievable assurance, experiencing yet again his unshakeable confidence in me as a person. (What a guy!)

Eventually, the conversation completely ground to a halt, and after a few uncomfortable minutes, I knew it was time to go. As I got up to leave and said goodbye, there was still no reaction from Mrs. Solomon, although her husband gave me a gracious enough farewell.

Aaron walked me to the door, holding my hand when his parents weren't looking and signing that I was to come back after my meeting. Needless to say, the Bible study went on without me, as all I could do was go over and over in my mind the last dreadful quarter of an hour, regretting every gesture I had made and every word I had spoken.

With the meeting over, I fled back to Aaron's apartment to hear the verdict. Well, much to my absolute amazement, Aaron's precious Abba had said he could see what Aaron saw in me—whatever that meant! All his mom could muster was, "Well, you have got to do something about the way she dresses!"

It was then that I realized that I could never feel a part of these people if I carried on looking the way I did. A sudden urge came over me to start looking like a Jewish lady and not like some gypsy out of Africa! Aaron's wise and probably unintended psychology had worked. In life you can never change anyone until they want to change themselves. His unconditional love had won the day, making me want to conform, bringing peace rather than strife into our lives. But my journey of love and self-sacrifice had just begun.

TWELVE

We thought, "Why wait any longer?" and started to think along the lines of my studying Judaism. I had already learned mounds by just being a part of Aaron's life, but we had to go the legal route and apply for "conversion." After all, this was Israel and the laws of the land, our master. After many phone calls, a date was set for me to visit a rabbi whose job it was to find out exactly why I wanted to convert. I can't explain how inconceivably difficult the whole process was, and, believe me when I say that I would not wish it on anyone. The humiliation, the questions, and the suspicion can crack you up to the point where you begin to doubt whether you have done the right thing. Which is exactly what the authorities want to achieve!

I was finally sent off for a weekend to a religious kibbutz outside Tiberius, where I was given a chance to taste the real thing for myself. I arrived by bus and was graciously welcomed by a large, typically Jewish family. They were getting ready for Shabbat. Not being a novice at this anymore, I also prepared in good Jewish style, which just confused the family who were wondering why I was there if I knew so much already. Anyway, it was a pleasant time up until I made the most shocking discovery.

It started when I noticed that the lady of the household looked very familiar. It was only until halfway through the evening meal, and during a conversation, that it dawned on me that she was none other than a close relative of Aaron's mother! I went cold and struggled to finish my meal.

What if they found out who the stranger was among them? Everyone had heard about "poor" Aaron, and about this "evil woman" who had a hold on him. Little did they know that *she* was in their midst! I could not handle much more for fear of being discovered, and so the next day, before the Sabbath had even ended, I politely excused myself and requested to return to Jerusalem before it got too dark—any excuse would do.

Aaron, of course, was both shocked and amused by the bizarre turn of events. The Lord, we thought, had a dangerous sense of humor that I could have done without this time around.

Soon after my return from Aaron's relatives, the harassment from the authorities picked up again. My phone was bugged and rang at unearthly hours. Every day my post was opened and the contents strewn on the apartment foyer floor. The hornet's nest had been stirred again, but somehow we knew it was not by his family. Something else was going on and my old fears came flooding back just like before: "Oh, Lord, are we two fools in love, having no business being together?"

One day, just before lunch, a Jewish man entered my little art studio, and casually looked around, admiring the few paintings on display. Nothing seemed out of the ordinary, as he politely inquired about the prices of this and that. I knew only too well that if you were unable to get a working visa, earning money in any country was illegal. However, after leaving the Embassy, where I had been on the usual volunteer's visa, I had neglected to change mine, thus leaving myself wide open for an offense that the authorities were so madly looking for. Unbeknown to me, this "art lover" had been sent to investigate me. By 2 p.m. that afternoon I was ordered to: "Shut down shop and appear before the Minister of the Interior with immediate effect!"

I was also told that I had neglected to respond to the many "summonses" that had been served against me. Summonses? What summonses? I suddenly realized that they must have been intercepted and removed from my post box. But I had no proof of this and I appeared to be without defense.

Once again I dashed off in a flood of tears to poor Aaron for support and advice. But this time he couldn't come up with a solution. I would have to stand before the court as demanded, and take it from there. "Oh, Lord, help!"

A Mr. Cohen was the man I had to see in the Jewish part of downtown Jerusalem. After much searching I found the building and entered its dark foyer only to find the lift broken. My legs were like jelly and could hardly cope with the three-floor ascent. With all the moisture in my mouth gone, I finally read "Mr. Cohen" on a very dark brown door, and feebly knocked, only to be ordered, *"Rega!"*

I collapsed onto an old bench outside the door to await further instructions. I felt like I was sitting on Death Row. Eventually I heard another muffled order. Gathering it was directed at me, I stumbled up and gingerly opened the door and walked into a room straight out of the movies: bookshelves reaching to the sky in a smoky haze and filing cabinets spilling their contents everywhere. Behind the huge desk, which could hardly be seen for papers, ashtrays, and fruit peels, I spotted Mr. Cohen. He was a little man in his early sixties with a long grey beard, bushy eyebrows, and pasty skin.

Without a word, he continued peeling an apple while I stood in front of him like a naughty child. Then, through sheer nerves, I slid down into the chair opposite him and awaited my fate. Noisily he continued eating his apple, not giving me even the slightest acknowledgement. After what felt like hours and in slow motion, he stood up and with much difficulty tried to maneuver his way to one of the many cabinets behind him.

He eventually turned around with a file in his hand and made his slow way back, thoughtfully fingering through the thick wad of paper. Then, without warning, he furiously slammed the file down on his desk and for a few seconds I could hardly see him for flying dust and ash. Then he bellowed, "Who are you? Why don't you leave us Jews alone and go home and marry a Catholic?"

His eyes were wild with fury, no doubt fueled by the countless people he had to chase away to protect his nation. If it was not the terrorists, it was the missionaries, so even nearing retirement, he applied himself to his job zealously.

Methodically and very angrily, he took me through the last three months of my life. The wad of paper was a meticulous report of all my movements. "You are like a Swiss clock!" he continued, obviously confused and irritated by my punctuality for my meetings, both Jewish and Christian. This is when he seemed to lose it and with a face contorted with rage shouted, *"What do you want from us Jews? Go home and leave us alone!"*

I had absolutely nothing to say to this barrage and this just seemed to infuriate him more, *"You are, from today, officially deported. Get out! Get out!"*

אם ימשו החקים האלה
מלפני נאם ה גם זרע ישראל ישבתו
מהיות גוי לפני כל הימים
אם ימדו שמים מלמעלה כה אמר ה
גם אני אמאס בכל
זרע ישראל על כל
אשר עשו נאם ה
ויחקרו מוסדי ארץ למטה

THIRTEEN

*M*y mind and body began to shut down as I reeled out of Mr. Cohen's office. I don't remember how I got home, but the next thing I knew Aaron was beside me. He waited patiently over the next few days as I tried to come to terms with what had just happened.

But Aaron refused to listen to my lamentations. He was an Israeli fighter, don't forget, who had attained everything he set his mind to—apart from stopping the divorce that his ex-wife initiated. So, to him, our situation was just another typically tough Israeli experience worth fighting for. "Cheer up, Liz! This isn't the end; it's just the beginning!"

Horrible thoughts haunted me about Aaron's motive for fighting. Was he just behaving like a spoiled child, wanting what he couldn't have? Or was it a righteous fight for what was truly his? How was I ever going to know?

In a strange way, the thought of leaving was quite a relief. Surely we would then be able to review our relationship from a more realistic and objective perspective. Was all the excitement and trauma of the past months blinding me to something? Was the test of our love about to begin or was it the beginning of the end?

Thanks to half a Valium a day, and Aaron's dogged faith, I drifted on, with hardly enough energy to breathe, let alone deal with the reality of what was actually happening. It was all too much to bear when blessed Jerusalem, its sights, sounds, and magical colors would have to be left behind—perhaps forever.

Nobody who has had the privilege of living in this divine city, and fallen in love with her, could handle being told, "You will never return!" She has an eternal pull that is so real that no authority other than God Himself can tell you this. I knew deep inside that some day I would return. For now my body had to go, but I knew that my heart would remain. Jerusalem was my home and nobody could take her away from me.

Thanks to Aaron's contacts, I was graciously given an extended three weeks to pack up and leave. But no matter how hard Aaron fought, the dreaded day finally came.

On a day that was too beautiful for two lovers to part, I took my pathetic-looking cases over to Aaron's apartment, from where we were going to leave for the airport. While Aaron did a few last minute things, I made one more good-bye call to a friend. As I put down the phone, I spotted a man peering through the bedroom window. To make sure I wasn't imagining things, I quietly crouched down to see better, and saw three plain clothed men with guns!

In absolute shock, I scurried in a half crouch to find Aaron, who, in one swift motion, shoved me behind the door and grabbed his own pistol from a nearby drawer. As quietly and skillfully as a cat, he ran to lock the balcony door, then motionlessly we crouched together behind his bedroom door, our hearts racing.

Aaron's mind raced even faster, wondering what he could possibly have done to deserve armed men surrounding his home. He then heard one of the men say that he could see my luggage in the lounge. Aaron sighed with relief. "Don't worry, I think it's just our usual shadows making sure that you're actually leaving."

A relieved Aaron hugged me and we smiled at each other as we realized how silly we must have looked behind the door. But we were very pleased that the armed men were just the regulars and not someone else with a more deadly motive.

It was a miracle that we were still able to laugh. We saw all we had been through as worth it because of our love. We believed that we shared a common destiny that made everything else pale in comparison. Love was going to conquer all.

The early evening *sherut* trip to Ben Gurion Airport was a nightmare and I couldn't bring myself to look up and see my beloved Jerusalem fading into the distance. I sobbed uncontrollably into Aaron's lap, not caring how it looked or sounded to the other passengers.

At the airport we had the usual two-hour wait before the international flight. It was far more bitter than sweet.

As time grew short, we hastily promised each other things we could not be sure of. We hugged and kissed, reminding each other that if He is for us, who can be against us?

Time ticked by and we clung to each other, hoping to transfer by osmosis the love that was consuming us. The three men with guns were there, too, waiting and watching, and I wondered if even they didn't have a lump in their throats as they witnessed the tragic scene. I'll never know, but believing how "dangerous" I was, they were taking no chances, and the strictest precautions had been taken to make sure I got on that plane.

The final call came, and Aaron tried to drown it out with wild kisses and hugs that almost crushed the bones in my back and face. No words can describe the final parting.

Once aboard the plane I passed out in a faint from nothing less than a broken heart. Would I ever see my Jerusalem or beloved Aaron again?

FOURTEEN

*A*s the plane flew over my home town of East London in the Eastern Cape of South Africa, I wondered how I was ever going to face my family. They were so far removed from my life in Israel. How could they ever know what I had tasted, seen, heard and fallen in love with? It was not just with a man, but with a culture, a way of life, a country, a people, and a place. And what would they think of the Messianic Judaism I had now adopted?

I stepped off the plane in a complete daze, and only barely noticed my mom and step-dad, Harry (known to my sisters and me as 'Uncle Har'), smiling and waving in the arrival lounge. They were thrilled to see me and couldn't wait to hear all my news. But from the look on my face they could see that this hadn't been one of my usual jaunts. There would be no ten-to-the-dozen commentary about this place and that person as my mom flipped through volumes of photographs.

My mom just pulled me into her maternal arms as Uncle Har stood by nervously, looking concerned. I couldn't hold back my tears any longer and sobbed into my mother's chest. Obviously deeply troubled herself, she chose the age-old parental tactic of distraction, hoping that if she took my mind off my problems, they would go away.

Once the car was packed and we were heading into town, I got a full weather update from her for the last year. "You know, my love, it's been so dry in the Eastern Cape, and if it doesn't rain soon, we'll have to have water restrictions. And you know what that means? That's right, I won't be able to water the garden, and you know my roses just crave water. It'll be a disaster! I'm praying about it every day, but so far the Lord hasn't answered. And as for poor Mrs. Taylor's azaleas ..." My head spun.

I could hardly believe that so little had changed in three years. As we rounded the corner into our neigborhood, the same old dog ran out barking at the same old cars driving past the same little houses with the unpainted garden walls.

Somewhere at the back of my mind, I could hear my mom prattling on about this one and that one on our road. Even Mrs. Brown got a mention and how well her children had done and how she talks non-stop about all their achievements on the sports field, boring everyone. Oh, and the new German couple that moved in around the corner seemed very nice, but my mom found it very odd that she could never see any windows open in the mornings when driving past. She reasoned that different cultures were very peculiar and that I had better be very sure of what I was to do with regards to all of *that*.

This was the first clue she gave me that she had actually received my letters from Israel, and knew just what was going on in my life. But, like a prize skater, she avoided that part of the ice. Uncle Har tried to keep the balance by reassuring me that my mother *did* keep quiet sometimes—when she was asleep!

As we approached our beautiful Bonnie Doon home on an avenue lined with exquisite Bauhinia trees (they were doing well in spite of the drought), Mom noticed that Dawn and Brian, our next-door neighbors, were home. "I'm sure they'd love to see you after all this time. Why don't you pop around and say hi before you unpack? They're so fond of you, Liz, and with Dawn being Catholic, she finds your whole Jewish discovery thing *so* interesting and I'm sure she could give you some advice."

I didn't know what to say, but fortunately Uncle Har helped me out. "For crying out loud, Rusty, leave the kid alone. The Snells are not running away. Surely they can wait until tomorrow to see her!"

"Thanks, Uncle Har," I said gratefully, and after grabbing a bag or two, retreated into the sanctuary of my childhood home.

So here I was. In three years I had fallen in love with the cream of Israeli society, been saturated by Jewish culture, been on the cutting edge of spiritual warfare in the most intense spiritual melting pot on earth, been hunted by secret agents, and in short, been totally changed. Now I had to go back to my past life in little old East London. I just couldn't bear it.

It was as though I had new ears and eyes, and nothing sounded or looked like I remembered it. It all seemed so superficial compared to my vibrant life in Israel. I no longer felt like I belonged in sunny South Africa, and I hated myself for feeling this way, knowing how much hurt I was causing my family.

Pain and depression followed me wherever I went— dreading the days and crying the nights away. The only thing that meant anything to me was thousands of miles away. The telephone became my lifeline for the next few months as just hearing Aaron's voice renewed my strength. Besides the weekly calls, Aaron proved to be one of the most amazing letter writers I have ever known. About every three days an Israeli stamped letter arrived—proof enough for any girl to know that he was serious!

Even with the comfort of knowing that I was truly loved, I was still hell to be with. Just like his parents, mine were also praying that in time I would settle down and give up my dream to go back to Israel and be with Aaron. I knew though that they felt my pain, and in a way I was quietly grateful for my mom's romantic heart. She was as heartbroken as I was and cried almost as much—it helped. My pain became hers as she tried to help me carry the load.

Unfortunately, thanks to the Eastern Cape bush telegraph, my story soon spread around the city of East London, and every Tom, Dick, or Harry offered my poor mom their penny's worth of doubtful Jewish conversion stories. For example: "Do you know how terrible it is for a new convert to feel a part of their new family, especially if they are the religious sort?"

Or, "Do you know that she'll have to wear a head-covering in public for the rest of her life?" This one was too much for Mom to handle and she burst into tears at the very thought of it. "What about your beautiful hair?" she wailed, "No one will ever see it again! You're so lively and fun-loving! How will you ever cope with such a rigid lifestyle? Please, my love, don't do it, *don't* do it!"

Soon neither my mother nor I could take it anymore, and I decided, for pure sanity's sake, to move to Cape Town. My dearest sister Shelagh was only too happy to have me back, as we used to share our family apartment in the city a few years before. It was going to be like old times.

Cape Town had always been my "next best" city after Jerusalem, and grace seemed to be with me at last. Life in the Cape Town suburb of Sea Point was a bit like living in Tel Aviv with the many Jewish people, familiar bagel delis, synagogues, and the unique vibe that only Jews can bring. So I did not feel too far removed from Jerusalem, even though Sea Point was ever so secular and unorthodox, compared to the Holy City. Perhaps here I would find direction and eventually start my long, but worthwhile journey back to Aaron again.

My darling fiancée continued with his fountain of calls and letters, tirelessly planning our strategy to be together again. Gradually my zest for life and our future together returned, and I began to seriously plan with Aaron how I was going to convert.

Remembering my past trauma, even just the thought of a rabbi made me cringe, but it had to be done—I had to make contact with the Rabbinical Court in Cape Town. But what if the Rabbinical Court in Jerusalem had contacted the Rabbinical Court here, warning them of this "Bride of Israel"? All our hopes would be dashed again, and what then?

But Aaron soon put my pessimism to rest with his words of encouragement and urged me to make the call. I did, and was amazed to be invited to make an appointment to discuss my conversion. Perhaps the Jerusalem court hadn't contacted them after all!

I soon found out that dealing with Orthodox Rabbinical Courts anywhere in the world is exactly the same—without patience, you'll go mad! After the first exciting call, weeks turned into months before I could even get to see the secretary to make an appointment. The secretary then set a date that was again months away before I could see the Board of Deputies.

It took the best part of a year to finally get to see anyone of any importance, and I soon realized that this was all part of the strategy. You see, Judaism has never encouraged conversion. The Jews believe that it is hard enough for Gentiles to live by the Ten Commandments (which they recognize were given not just to them, but to the rest of the world) without having to deal with the other six hundred and thirteen laws that they must live by. To any logical mind, it was questionable that Gentiles would want to encumber themselves with a way of life that they were not born to.

The orthodox conversion process was made so difficult that only someone who was really serious, or felt called by God, would push through to the end. I believed that I was.

Nine long months went by before I darkened the Rabbinical Court door, during which time I kept busy working part-time as a waitress and painted after-hours in preparation for an exhibition.

The waiting seemed pointless to me as I already felt Jewish and had always looked Jewish. I had even experienced anti-Semitism.

I remembered how years ago at art school when I chose Jerusalem as a theme for a few art works, I discovered that the monster of anti-Semitism was still alive and well. Knowing I was not even Jewish, a certain lecturer started showing incredible animosity towards everything I did with regard to Israel. He also belittled me constantly about my love for the country and my desire to go back and live there. One day when we were alone in the studio, he actually hit me across my back for something so trivial that I knew it was actually a manifestation of the spirit of anti-Semitism. I remembered that, as the Bible says, the battle is not against flesh and blood but against powers and principalities in the spirit realm. So I backed off, realizing that his anger was not actually directed at me personally, but at the God of Israel who resided in me by His Spirit.

This was the start of my consciousness of the very real enemy that the Jewish people are still up against. I felt that Hashem allowed this to happen to show me the enemy so that I could identify with what the Jewish people had to suffer. Having little idea at the time of how significant this experience would be, I know now why it happened, and count it a privilege to be enlightened and counted as one with Israel.

I could now relate, in even the smallest way, with the suffering of the Jews throughout history from a result of anti-Semitism. We've seen it manifested from far back in history with the Pharaohs in Egypt, the Spanish Inquisition, the pogroms, Hitler, and most ashamedly, for me as a Christian, the Crusaders. These misled zealots marched under big gold crosses, the symbol of our beloved Messiah, slaughtering the "Christ Killers" in the name of Christianity. All of them were tools in the hand of the enemy to rid the earth of the very race that God had chosen to usher in salvation for the world. But they had failed, and in due course, God Himself will crush this anti-Semitic spirit that will use any tool or people group available, and He will eventually lift Israel and Jerusalem up to be praised in all the earth. This is His Word and it will be fulfilled whether we like it or not, and I felt that my small life was to be a part of accomplishing this.

FIFTEEN

It took almost a year before a date was set for me and other potential converts to appear before a panel of Jewish Deputies. This was just a questioning session to ascertain why on earth we would want to take on all the Jewish laws when we could remain as we were! Then, only once they had thought it through for as long as they deemed fit, were we contacted by post and informed whether or not we were considered worthy to commence with the course.

There must have been about twelve of us in that intake. Judging by what I saw, I could sympathize a little with the Court and the decisions they would have to make. The jewelry, hairstyles and clothing—all the height of fashion—made it clear that the majority of candidates had no real interest in Judaism, but each had obviously met a "nice Jewish boy." A few were already pregnant, which for them would obviously help sway the final decision. Lucky them!

Although I had also met a "nice Jewish boy," my situation was different. Finally, my turn came, and I walked determinedly through the perfumed haze to the interviewing room beyond.

In response to the first question about why I wanted to convert, I gushed, "Well, to tell you the Gospel truth, (whoops!) I have fallen in love with the way of life and want it with or without Aaron, my fiancée!"

Blushing profusely, I then, with much conviction, shared with them my wonderful discovery of Judaism. It flowed out like water from a fresh spring. The deputies were wide-eyed and I knew I had touched their hearts and found favor.

Eventually, after a too-long wait, I received a letter congratulating me on being accepted. I was disappointed to see that I would only be allowed into the following year's intake, but I was "in" and that was all that mattered.

At the back of my mind, though, I could not help feeling suspicious and wondering whether this was another awful trick. After all, it only took a phone call from Israel to warn the South African authorities here. It seemed to be going all too smoothly for me, and as before, I anticipated a backlash of some kind.

But nothing untoward happened and eventually the long-awaited course arrived—what a disappointment! We went at a snail's pace, and I thought I was going to pass out from frustration and boredom. Being such a mixed bag of people, and at different levels of understanding, the rabbi in charge obviously had to start at the very beginning. Pure frustration made me call one of the other rabbis and tell him how I felt. Much to my relief, he understood me completely, and promptly set about making plans to exempt me from the classes.

The cherry on top was when he personally offered to put me through my paces. My prayers had been answered—I was in the home stretch.

His family became mine and I became like another daughter to them. As time passed and I continued to grow in my knowledge of the Jewish way, I was entrusted to collect distinguished guest-rabbis from the airport. I was expected to drive them around the poor townships of Cape Town where the Jewish community had helped to set up children's creches and other charitable works. My smattering of Hebrew was well tested during these exciting trips.

I was also thrilled that Aaron and I were rapidly heading towards our goal of being together again. He, to say the least, was delighted by the wonderful progress I was making and very grateful to my new "adopted family."

Passover arrived and I was honored to be invited to the chief rabbi of Cape Town's home for the *Seder*. Hardly believing the favor I had found, I was naturally excited, yet extremely nervous at the same time. Being among the cream of the Jewish community in South Africa after my past experiences was a miracle! Life was never just normal for me, always going from the sublime to the ridiculous, and now, here I was off to the chief rabbi's for *Pesach*!

Fortunately I was well acquainted with the Passover, thanks to Aaron and his methodical teaching, and found the whole historical deliverance story astounding.

You must know how it can be, Jewish readers, when you faithfully do something every year—it can become a tradition and the wonder of the miracle can fade. But not for me; it was just amazing to know that the God of Israel has been faithful to every promise He made to Abraham, Isaac, and Jacob, and today the state of Israel is living proof of it.

No other nation has had the privilege of having the very God of the Universe as its keeper. It was a subject I loved, and now, the wonderfully significant customs and traditions would be played out during Pesach to remind us of God's miraculous deliverance of the Jews from slavery out of Egypt.

I also discovered that this was when Yeshua was crucified some two thousand years ago to the very hour, spiritually delivering the world from its slavery to sin. I questioned why Christians called the festival "Easter," and not "Pesach." Why was the Church not following the Jewish calendar and its festivals anymore? Where did they get their festivals if Jesus the Jew said that He did not come to abolish the Law, but to fulfill it?

My thankfulness to Hashem was now two-fold: firstly for the physical deliverance of the Jews out of Egypt, and secondly for the spiritual deliverance of all mankind from its slavery to sin when Yeshua became the Passover Lamb and was slain for the world.

With Judaism, I discovered that the festivals were celebrated in slightly different ways in all the countries where the Jews had settled, but the essence was always the same, bringing unity to a dispersed people.

I could imagine Aaron celebrating with his family in Israel, we in South Africa, and many others all over the globe, united in one spirit. These celebrations I came to understand are what has kept the Jewish people and their customs alive through the centuries and why God commanded them to be remembered. Together with the unity they bring, they are a yearly reminder of God's faithfulness and redemption plan for the whole of mankind. I was in awe of His wisdom.

In the rabbi's dining room, special Passover crockery and cutlery were used, and the large oval table was set for a king. The Seder platters were laden with their symbolic foods, and delicious aromas wafted in from the very busy kitchen.

One by one, the Passover dishes were laid on the table, including the *matzah*, wine, and salt water. The *seder* plate contains bitter herbs, roasted egg, a roasted shank bone, a brown mixture called *harosset*, and green vegetables known as *karpass*. All of the food is tasted in its turn as the evening progresses, becoming a living reminder of the story of Passover. For example, the bitterness of the moror (horseradish) calls to mind the bitterness of the slavery in Egypt. The salt water is a reminder of the tears shed during this time, and the roasted egg of the new life that is to come.

There were eighteen guests expected that night, so you can well imagine the size of this gorgeous table. We all sat in our designated places. Beside me, on my right, was the dearest old man, Sabba, with a wizened Jewish face. He was ninety years old and hailed from

Lithuania—a delightful character with whom I fell in love immediately. I was told by other guests to speak loudly and clearly, because his hearing had gone years ago.

The rabbi's youngest son on my left was horribly neglected, but from our occasional smiles at each other, I knew that he understood my fascination with the older man. I discovered that Sabba had been a rabbi for many years in Lithuania, but since his retirement had been living here in South Africa.

Throughout the Seder I would occasionally glance in the old man's direction to see whether he needed any help, when, to my embarrassment, I would catch him just staring at me. The rabbi's son, along with everyone at the table, found it very amusing and I was told that by this stage of the Seder, Sabba was usually sound asleep and snoring in his chair. I obviously was a big hit and well worth staying awake for!

During the main course, Sabba leaned over to me and with his thick accent in a stage whisper asked, "So ven is your fiancée going to convert?"

Taken aback, I replied, "No, Sabba, I am the one who has to convert, not my fiancée!"

To which he replied, in disbelief, "Nooo! You are Jewish, you look Jewish, you talk Jewish. God must have made a mistake!"

Smilingly, I turned to my host, the chief rabbi, and said "Sabba, you tell the rabbi that!" Everyone exploded with laughter as the little man sat back, confounded.

And so the process of my conversion to Judaism continued. One morning in shul I learned, rather rudely, that I couldn't just sit where I liked. Certain seats are unofficially "reserved" the whole year around for certain people (usually the elderly), regardless of whether they are there or not. If you are unfortunate enough to be caught sitting in that particular seat on their arrival, you are publicly rebuked.

I soon discovered a "safe place" next to a lovely elderly lady named Bella, who didn't care if people sat in the "wrong" seats or not. She and I became good shul friends and she called me her angel as I often helped her find her place in the book. One day we were sitting together when Bella struck me with the most unexpected question imaginable. She looked me straight in the eye and in a loud voice asked, "Elizabeth, are you Jewish?" Immediately I looked down to where the rabbi was sitting and, horror of horrors, he was looking straight up at us. Judging by his expression, I could see he was saying, "Please, ladies, won't you keep quiet for once?"

Still stunned and desperately trying to work out how to reply to Bella's surprising question, she pointed at my face and made the most extraordinary statement: "Because I see Jesus in your eyes, and don't you let that rabbi tell you anything else. He is the Son of God, you know, the Son of David, Messiah!" She continued, pointing to the rabbi, "They think I've gone senile, but I haven't. No, no, no, I tell you, I haven't!"

As you can imagine, Bella and I became even better friends after we had discovered our shared faith, and wondered just how many other people secretly believed in "Him."

Another amazing thing happened when I decided to attend a three-part lecture delivered by a Professor Davidson on the subject of "Can Judaism and Secularism Mix?" I was entranced by the professor's eloquence and amazed by his unbelievable knowledge. All was going well until the final lecture. He said he felt that in this day and age of free thought and expression, maybe the Jews ought to start thinking about allowing their children to choose for themselves which path they would like to follow. Hopefully, with good parenting and God willing, they would eventually choose Judaism in the end.

Immediately the hairs stood up on the back of my neck, and, together with a couple of other Orthodox people, we voiced our disapproval, only to be told by the lecturer to hold our horses as there would be time at the end of the lecture for discussion. Boy, what a discussion it was!

Everyone and his dog had an opinion delivered with such passion and conviction that it was nearly impossible to get a word in. But the longer it went on, the more my heart was pounding in my chest, which was a sign to me that I wouldn't be able to keep my mouth shut for long.

"Oh, Lord, help, here I go!" I found a gap and shot up my hand. With my heart in my mouth, and blushing madly, I began by saying, "I can probably say this only because I am not born Jewish"—at which the whole hall turned around to see who it was.

Undaunted, I continued, "How on earth can you say that you should let your children choose for themselves, when the very Word of God tells you to teach your children in the ways of the Lord, and then they will not depart from them?"

Then, a friend who was with me could not contain herself either. She jumped up and said, "Yes, are you wanting to move the goalposts of God's laws to suit the world and yourselves? Whose standards are you Jews supposed to live by, God's or this rotten world's?" Well, we received a standing ovation from all the religious folk, and shocked looks from the rest.

At the tea break, we were surrounded by scores of people congratulating us and wanting to know who we were. I then noticed a slightly built, elderly lady beckoning madly for me to come and chat with her. When I did, she rolled up her sleeve, revealing a horrible Holocaust number tattooed on her arm. Before I could say a word, she told me that her name was Paula and that she was from Italy. She then proceeded to tell me a story that reduced me to tears—not from sadness, as expected, but from the utter wonder of the reality and faithfulness of our God.

She had been captured, like millions of others, and kept like an animal in a concentration camp. She explained how she and her fellow prisoners used to take turns sleeping for a few hours at a time in the too-few bunk beds. One night, while it was her turn to sleep, she was awakened by a bright light. Knowing there were no lights in her cell, she was startled and sat up to see what was going on. There at the end of the bed, before her eyes, sat a "man" in bright shining clothes.

As she told me the story, she placed her hands over her face, stroking her wrinkled cheeks. With great love in her eyes, she said, "And He had a beard, and I know that you know who He was! He was Yeshua, the Messiah!"

Yeshua told her that after the war, she was to go and find out more about Him through "true believers." He also said that when the Gentile believers, like myself, and the Jewish people say together: "*Blessed is He who comes in the Name of the Lord*," His Second Coming would be imminent. Meeting people like my friend and I made her very excited, and she hoped that just maybe He would come in her lifetime!

These encounters, I believe, were sent to encourage me and teach me that the secret mysteries of our God are revealed to the simple like myself and dear old Paula and Bella.

I was thinking about these things when I received the usual phone call from Israel. My heart leaped at the thought of talking to my beloved, but only moments into the conversation I collapsed in a chair, with the phone dangling from my hand. It was devastating news: Aaron, my Aaron, was getting married—but not to me!

SIXTEEN

When I heard Aaron's voice, I knew immediately that something was horribly wrong. All he could muster in a stammering voice was, "I-I-I've got to make a decision, Liz!" A decision! What kind of decision could cause Aaron so much distress? Nothing ever seemed to catch him off-guard or upset him. "What decision, Aaron?" I asked nervously, not sure that I wanted to know.

"I have to decide whether or not to go back to my wife." "Your wife? But you're divorced."

"Yes, I know, but it's not as easy as that." "Why not?" I asked, confused.

And so, he began to tell me. With me out of the country, Aaron's ex-wife had had enough time (and plenty of family pressure) to realize that she had made a mistake in divorcing Aaron—now she wanted him back. According to Jewish law, if children are involved, all lengths are gone to get the family together again.

So there was poor Aaron, torn between a life with me or being reunited with his little ones and becoming a family again. What a hideous dilemma!

This is when I had to marvel at true love. Here I had been, a few months earlier, wondering if I would ever be able to love Aaron unconditionally, without always considering my own selfish needs, when—BANG—here was my test! I was going to have to put myself in his shoes and try to understand what he was going through.

Having learned that true love never demands its own way, and rejoices in the truth, I was sorely challenged. How could I want anything else but what ultimately was best for him? Thoughts of my own needs evaporated.

I suddenly had a flashback from twenty or so years before when my own parents went through a divorce, and I recalled the deep sorrow in my five-year-old heart of no longer having my daddy come home anymore. The anger and feeling of wanting to hurt someone for causing this pain came flooding back. Aaron's little boy of six came before my mind's eye, and it was then I knew I dared not stand in the way of this family's second chance.

I'm starting to sound like Mother Theresa here, and can imagine what you might be thinking! But truly, real sacrificial love took over and the high price that it demands was being paid. The old cliché, "If you love something, let it go; if it comes back to you, it's yours, but if it doesn't, it never was," was going to have to prove itself. Aaron could hardly believe my response, and I will never know whether he felt hurt or relieved.

God had performed a miracle in my heart, allowing me to let the love of my life go. Aaron had to go back to where he belonged. And me? Well, God would have to sort that out.

Our goodbye was impregnated with so much respect and understanding that in a crazy way I still felt deeply loved and honored. Oddly, in being granted the privilege of knowing true love and being enabled by God to let my fiancée go back to the woman of his youth, I was victorious. But I won't pretend that I wasn't in pain—I was in agony.

Soon salt was poured into my very raw wounds, as toxic remarks began to fly: "I told you so. He was just on the rebound." "What do they say? Out of sight out of mind!" "Shame, poor Liz, imagine how dumped she must feel!" "What deception, to believe that he would ever have married her!" "Poor girl, a thing like this could affect her for life, you know!"

These assumptions were more hurtful than what had actually happened. My dear sister Shelagh became a tower of strength to me, even taking time off work to be with me. In a way it felt like Aaron had died, and naturally I was grieving. Yes, I was at peace with the decision I had made, but I still had to deal with the pain.

At that time, my sister was one of the many secretaries for Pik Botha, then Minister of Foreign Affairs for South Africa. He happened to overhear her explaining to the girls in the office my tragic love story and the reasons for taking time off work. Led by compassion for me, he asked my sister if I would like to join them at a dinner party the following evening at his Newlands home.

As I told my sister, hobnobbing with South Africa's top brass was the last thing I wanted to do. Under different circumstances, though, I would have leaped at the chance to peek into the hornet's nest of right wing politics. The ruling party in South Africa in the late 1980s (as it had been since 1948) was the right wing National Party who developed the insane policy of Apartheid to a fine art. I was much more leftist leaning in my politics and was proud to have voted for the anti-Apartheid Democratic Party in the last election. But the white leaders of the time were a "colorful" bunch nonetheless, and an evening in their company would be intriguing.

At least, that is, before Aaron left me. Now all I could think of was him and the love that we had shared—dolling up for a party wasn't on my agenda. "Besides, I have nothing to wear," I told my sister as she scratched through my wardrobe, refusing to take no for an answer. I had lost so much weight due to grief, that nothing seemed to fit me anymore, and I lay on my bed in too-loose slacks, thinking that that was that.

"Then you can just wear something of mine," said Shelagh firmly. Another hour of arguing did nothing to dissuade her, and I somehow found myself in the passenger seat of her car in a sleek little number.

Soon we pulled up the oak-lined avenue to Mr. Botha's Cape Dutch home and were greeted by polished guards who opened the enormous gates. We drove through magnificent gardens, sporting the uniquely beautiful Western Cape fynbos, indigenous to this part of the world. Our doors were opened and we were ushered up a graceful, terracotta staircase into the picture-perfect house, decked out like a museum. But tell-tale touches of domesticity, like a well-used coat stand and a boisterous dog, told me that this impressive house was also a home.

The minister himself greeted us in his husky voice: "*Goeie naand, dames* (Good evening, ladies). Welcome Elizabeth, at last I meet the artist in person. Come! Come see where your painting is hanging above my desk in the study. I was so glad when your sister gave me this fishing boat painting as a present. I hope she paid you!" So, I unbelievably followed the laughing Mr. Botha, one of the most powerful men in the country, to see where my painting hung on his wall!

Then, the unexpectedly warm man led us into the dining room, lured by the smell of roast venison and guineafowl that he proudly told us he had shot himself!

The room was filled with people I had seen before only on television, including the ministers of defense and finance. I did my best not to embarrass my sister, as she had already told me that this was the National Party and not my "free radical liberal *gubbas* around a *lekker brraai.*" After chatting to some dignitaries, and minding my every word, I helped our gracious hostess, the late Mrs. Botha, clear the table.

Behind the kitchen door I was finally able to relax as I shared some jokes and nibbled on the leftovers with the household staff. But whether I was queen of the ball or Cinderella, the out-of-the-ordinary distraction was good for my broken heart. In fact, I almost never thought of my own Prince Charming, until the lights of Newlands were behind me again.

SEVENTEEN

Everyone said, "Time heals." I hated to hear it—
but it was true. The Rabbinical Court wisely advised
me to take a few months break from my studies, thus
giving me time to settle down and in due course decide
what to do.

Very few people convert to Judaism without a
marriage in sight, unless there are obvious deep religious
convictions that override everything else. I, of course,
had told the rabbis at my first interview that my primary
motivation for seeking conversion was spiritual, and
that my love for Aaron was a secondary thing. But they
and I knew that my claims had not yet been tested. So
here was the test, and my response blew my mind. My
desire to continue studying just grew and grew, and I
wanted, without a doubt, to still be a part of Israel and
her people, no matter what.

I felt I needed to stand and fight for what God has
given Israel and not to back down under political
pressure. I reasoned that as a Jewess, this would be easier,
and I had found a worthy cause to live and fight for.
This must have been *Hashem's* original plan for my life

with Aaron, the stepping-stone needed. Nothing would stop me from getting there now!

All of a sudden things started to make sense again. I was going to become like Golda Meir—Israel's one and only female Prime Minister of the past—and make a difference!

So, with my five months of healing completed, I returned to the Rabbinical Court, sure of my desire to continue. I told them very firmly what I had decided (being careful not to mention the Golda Meir bit) and was touched by their heart-warming response. To them this was a rare and genuine case of a "true convert," and they were thrilled.

Nothing can be more fulfilling in life than to have a goal and purpose, and I had found it. My original rabbi friend and his family were also overjoyed, and I was welcomed back into their lives with open arms. My life started again.

Every night after shul and the Shabbat meal, the rabbi and his young son would walk me home. It was on one such occasion that he said something that sent my heart and head spinning. The rabbi had an opinion that he had kept to himself, but on this night he decided to share it with me. It was his scepticism about Aaron and his remarriage: "I doubt very much if this second marriage of Aaron's will last, Liz, and I think you can get ready for another call from Israel!"

I didn't know what to say, so I mumbled a quick good-night, and ran into my apartment. Did he know something that I didn't? How dare he plant any kind of hope in my tender heart? How could he even say such a thing if he didn't have any hard evidence? No, it was out of the question, too much for me to even think about.

Over the next few days I became progressively more angry and disturbed, not knowing how to stop the million wild thoughts that were plaguing me. Hope deferred makes the heart sick—as the Torah states— and mine had been about as sick as it could get. Up until now I was extremely grateful to God for keeping me sane throughout the whole ordeal—I didn't need any more disruption to my tender soul.

Purim was the next celebration on the Jewish calendar, and I submerged myself in it, hoping that all thoughts of Aaron would be kept at bay. Purim is the festival written about in the biblical Book of Esther. In the story, Queen Vashti is dethroned because of her disobedience to her husband, King Ahasuerus. The king then orders a search to be made throughout the Persian Empire for the most beautiful women to parade before him so he could choose a new queen.

After many months of beauty therapy and preparation, Esther, the young and exquisite cousin of Mordecai—one of the exiled Jews from Nebuchadnezzar's campaign against Jerusalem—was chosen. Esther's Jewish identity had never been revealed, so when the Prime Minister, Haman, wanted a decree issued: destroy all the Jews in the Persian Empire (the monster of anti-Semitism again), the queen's life would be in danger if her ethnicity was exposed. Haman had made a law that all people had to bow down to him wherever he went. So when Mordecai did not do this because of the command that "you shall not worship (bow down to) any other god but me," Haman took offense.

Haman told the king that the Jews were "different" and would not obey him or the laws of the land. As punishment they should be done away with because of their "disrespect" for his authority. Haman threw a *pur* (a Persian word for lot or dice) to divine which day the Jews should be killed on.

The king agreed and signed an edict ordering the rulers of all the provinces in the empire to annihilate the Jews on the selected day in the twelfth month, the month of *Adar*.

In desperation, Mordecai contacted his cousin Esther and begged her to go before the king and plead on behalf of her people. Esther reminded Mordecai that no one, including the queen, could appear before the king without being personally invited by him—it could cost her life.

Mordecai responded: *"Do you think you will escape—there in the palace—where all other Jews are killed? If you keep quiet at a time like this, God will deliver the Jews from some other source, but you and your relatives will die. What's more, who can say but that God has brought you into the palace for just such a time as this?"*

Esther then requested that all of the Jews fast and pray for her so that she would find favor before the king to stop this horrendous act. She did, the Jews were saved, and Haman was hanged on the very gallows that he had prepared for Mordecai.

The story shows how the God of the Jews hears prayer and will never allow His people to be destroyed or kept from the destiny that He has prepared for them. So until this day the Jews celebrate the festival of *Purim* on the fourteenth day of Adar as a reminder of the time when Haman, the enemy of all the Jews, plotted to destroy them.

It was the perfect time for me to get involved, and I prayed God would also save me from being destroyed by my grief, as I tried to forget what the rabbi had said about Aaron. Israel and her people have a God-given destiny and I wanted to be a part of it. If only I could be as bold as Esther to say that God had called me for "such a time as this." I believed that God had a plan for my life, too, and it included helping to put Israel back in her rightful place.

As thoughts of what I imagined was my godly calling filled my mind, and I saw how I fit into the bigger picture, thoughts of Aaron began to dim. That is, until my telephone rang on that Purim morning in 1987 ...

EIGHTEEN

It was Aaron. Too shocked to get excited, I tried to keep control as a very traumatized man began to tell me in a few choice words about his "second" divorce! Crying—whether from relief or pain I couldn't tell—he humbly asked my forgiveness for the hurt he had caused.

"I'm so sorry, Liz, I'm so sorry. I ... I ... I ..." he stammered, but couldn't go on as he choked back the tears. He was obviously embarrassed by his reaction and realized the dilemma he had put me in. "Look, I understand if this is too much for you," he said, suggesting that I had a right to reject him; then: "Maybe we should hang up, and I'll call back later."

"No! Don't!" I half yelled down the phone, not wanting to be apart from my beloved for longer than was necessary. I tried to tell him how much I still loved him as hot tears surged down my cheeks. Weeping, we clung together on the line, not wanting to put down the phone for fear that our second chance would evaporate. Then I told him that I had continued with the conversion course and he was ecstatic. He never thought that I would carry on without him. This was the sign he needed.

"Don't worry, my love, we'll be together again," he said, as finally and reluctantly we hung up.

You can well imagine the party we had that Purim night! The Jewish community joined me in my ecstasy; my Aaron had returned.

Shortly after Purim, the rabbi's wife left for Israel on a month's sabbatical, and asked me to be "housekeeper" while she was away.

It seemed a great idea as their four children knew me well, and by then, with the help of their wonderful maid, I could keep a nice *kosher* home. So all was arranged, and she confidently set off, but not before I had given her all Aaron's details, pleading with her to meet up with him. I wanted to show him off, for her to see what a wonderful man he really was. Torah states that whenever a man finds a wife, he finds a "good thing." Well, it's the other way around, too, and I prayed that we would soon be each other's "good thing."

All was going well in the rabbi's household in South Africa when, during the second week of his wife's absence, we received another of her many calls. There was the usual flurry of excitement from the kids as one by one they chatted with Mom; then it was the rabbi's turn. He nodded and said, "Mmm, mmm" as he listened to his wife, and glanced at me a few times with a curious look on his face. Finally he said, "Yes, I agree totally, my dear. I will see what I can do."

A chill tingled down my spine as I thought that perhaps the rabbi's wife had heard something about me from the authorities in Israel. All I wanted to do was flee, but I was trapped in a breakfast nook with the rabbi and his children blocking my escape. Things appeared even more threatening when, after the call, the rabbi seemed unusually smug, as though he knew *everything.*

Worse was still to come when he said that I must put the children to bed early so we could "talk!" Pale-faced and parch-mouthed, I felt like a lamb being led to the slaughter. What did he know? What should I do?

After putting the children to bed, I came and sat down nervously on a kitchen stool. The rabbi was furiously looking up a number in the telephone directory. Oh no! He was going to contact the authorities! Why did my life have to be like this?

Then, totally out of the blue, the rabbi jumped to his feet, grabbed me by the shoulders in excitement, and said, "Why do you look so miserable—smile!"

"About what?" I asked feebly.

With a broad grin, the rabbi then proceeded to explain that his wife had met Aaron. In her opinion, it was crazy for us to carry on any longer the way we were when she could see what caliber of Jew he was. "She said that it's a sin to keep you apart any longer, and I agree!" said the rabbi triumphantly, as he started to dial.

"Who are you calling?"

"The Rabbinical Court, of course!"

"But why?"

"Because my wife said that we shouldn't waste any more time. We're going to get permission to set a wedding date!"

"A wedding date?"

"Yes, of course. You can't get married without setting a date, now can you? Now, before I call the chief rabbi, tell me which date would suit you," he said, pointing to a calendar on the door. "How about the ninth of August?"

At break-neck speed I did a quick calculation to check if I would be menstruating during that time, as Jewish couples are forbidden to have intercourse during a woman's monthly. Needless to say, a happy, uninterrupted honeymoon was essential! To my relief, August ninth was just fine, thank you very much!

I was still in a bit of daze when the rabbi suggested that we call Aaron to confirm the date with him. "Of course," I said, and then clumsily began to dial his number.

Aaron answered the phone and sounded delighted to hear my voice. But then, before I could tell him the good news, I burst into tears.

"What's wrong, my love?" he asked.

"N-n-nothing. It's just that ..." then more uncontrollable sobbing. Fortunately, the rabbi was a man of action and he pried the phone from my hand and told Aaron the good news himself. I simply sank back on my stool and contemplated the goodness of God. Aaron and I were finally going to be married!

NINETEEN

Now we knew that God was on our side and that when He opens doors, nobody can shut them. I never dreamed that it would happen so fast. Two short months was all we had to arrange invitations, a reception, dresses, flights to and from Cape Town, kosher caterers, *chuppa,* and general wedding arrangements.

My family and friends were as stunned as I was, but they rushed into top gear and did everything they could to help.

"Joanie, can you help with the flowers?"

"No problem, Liz."

"Charlotte, can you pick up the tickets from the travel agent?"

"Anything for you, Liz."

"Trudi, I need some shoes."

"Don't worry, I know just the place!"

This was going to be a wedding of a lifetime— nobody was going to miss *this* one.

My dear grandmother of eighty-five was the one with the most to say. She had always disapproved of cross-cultural marriages, so for her, this took the cake.

Eventually one day she burst out laughing and said, "Oh, well, what can I say, Liz? You people never want to listen, but at least he seems a nice boy!"

She had met Aaron once before when she and my parents had come over to Israel when I was working for the Christian Embassy. Never believing in a million years that we would ever marry one day, she had said, "What a nice fellow, pity he's Jewish!" So, coming to terms with the fact that she was now going to have a Jewish granddaughter and probably many little Jewish great-grandchildren took time for her to digest.

She, together with many other traditional Christians, saw no connection between her faith and that of the Jews, and could see no blessing in it. "Well, at least he's not a Muslim because then I would give up!" she added wryly.

Anyway, everything miraculously took shape, thanks to my amazingly capable friends. They just did it all, knowing that I was frantically busy with my final immigration documents and last minute meetings with the rabbis. What an incredible witness to me of how much they cared! The flowers, my outfit, and all the other finer details were as good as done, and I was so grateful, especially to my art school friends, Charlotte and Joan, for their initiative and creativity. Girls, that last-ditch attempt of yours to design my headgear was astounding! Right down to the color of the serviettes, I still marvel at it all. You truly get to know the depth of friends' care in times like these. All I can say is that I have been blessed with these two women who are worth more to me in my life than most things in this world.

By this time, my darling sister had been posted to the Embassy in Paris, so we no longer shared the flat. She was, obviously, hot on the line as often as she could to encourage me, regretting the fact that she couldn't be with me during this exciting time. She had grown very fond of Aaron during the early days of our courtship when he had become almost like a brother to her from all our contact. Then of course, she knew the degree of the love we shared.

It was all so unreal, each day zooming by as other people took control. But I didn't resent it, as all I was consumed with was Aaron's arrival! After two long years of being apart, I could hardly imagine how it would be.

However, there was one last very important task that nobody could do for me and this was to choose a Jewish couple to stand in proxy on behalf of Aaron's parents at the wedding.

Aaron had tried to convince his parents that I would make the perfect daughter-in-law after my conversion and that they would be pleasantly surprised at the "new me" despite all the horrible stories they had heard about me. But they weren't convinced, and refused to have anything to do with the wedding. Although Aaron was saddened by their attitude, he was a strong man with strong convictions, and nothing was going to stop him from marrying me.

So, he was coming to South Africa without his parents and I had to find a couple to stand proxy for them. This didn't take long; I knew exactly who they should be: Sheila and Ian, who had always made me feel part of the community to the point where I felt like their daughter. Sadly, Ian has now passed on, but I remain eternally grateful to them both. They were honored to accept the task.

With this done, the day of all days, the day when Aaron would arrive, was looming. No longer was the telephone going to be our lifeline and the bills sky-high, I would finally see him face-to-face. I would finally hear his voice as it really was, and not an electronic version of it. I would finally feel his lips and his hands and his strong arms around me. I would finally be able to lay my cheek on his chest and know that everything was going to be all right. Aaron was on his way!

That electrifying day arrived and the morning hours dragged past like weeks. I could not decide whether I was hot or cold from sheer nerves. As Aaron's plane taxied to a standstill at Cape Town airport, I waited with unbearable impatience to catch my first glimpse of him. I knew just what he would look like, how he would walk, the exact angle he would hold his head as he looked for me among the crowd. I had seen it in my dreams nearly every night for two years. But maybe I was wrong. Maybe he had changed, maybe I had forgotten him, maybe ... no, I wasn't wrong, there was my love walking down the gangway, just as I had remembered him.

Reaching the terminal entrance, he spotted me, dropped his hand luggage, and unashamedly ran into my arms. The rest of the airport disappeared—we saw nobody apart from each other, and noticed nothing except the feeling of our bodies entwined. Fused and trembling, we hugged and clung to each other until reality in the form of a porter, tapping Aaron on the shoulder, brought us back to the real world. Aaron's lonely suitcase was doing its hundredth round! Was it really that long that we were there, in heaven?

TWENTY

*T*o drive like a sober human being was my next task. The usual tour guide commentary—the famous Groote Schuur Hospital where the first heart transplant was held, the eland on the mountain slopes, Lion's Head and Table Mountain—was definitely out of the question, as all we could focus on was each other.

I even found it difficult to pry my hand from his to just change gears! By God's grace alone, we arrived at my apartment accident free, and spent the next two hours just "being" together, saying very little. We didn't need words—our spirits communicated on a different level. Eventually we had to come back down to earth and prepare ourselves for that night's appointment.

This day of the fourth August—five days before our wedding—coincided with *Tisha B'av* on the Jewish calendar. This explained why Aaron and every other observant Orthodox man in the world had a three-week beard growth and wore rubber-soled shoes instead of leather ones—it was a sign of mourning. This fast is the saddest day of the Jewish year. Both the First Temple (which King Solomon had built) and the Second Temple (which the returning exiles from Babylonia had rebuilt) were destroyed on this same date, hundreds of years apart. The First Temple fell to the Babylonians in the year 586 BC, and the Second Temple in 70 CE, following Judea's defeat in the war against Rome.

After the destruction of each of these temples, the Jews were driven from their land into exile: in 586 BCE to Babylonia, and in 70 CE into the Great Exile throughout the world, where they wandered for two thousand years. This punishment in itself would have been sufficient reason to make them mourn on Tisha B'av, but as if such a terrible blow was not enough for the Jews, a number of other tragic events occurred on the same date. Here are just a few of them:

1. The Israelites, following their Exodus from Egypt on the ninth of Av, were told that they would have to wander in the desert for forty years.

2. Betar, a powerful Jewish stronghold, fell to the Romans in 135 CE on the ninth of Av.

3. The Jews in Spain were expelled from that land on the ninth of Av in 1492 (just a few months before Columbus set sail for the New World).

4. The beginning of World War 1 in 1914 was on this day, too.

5. To top it all, it was on this day that Hitler was given permission to do as he pleased with the Jews, resulting in the Holocaust. No wonder the rabbis called this day, "a day set for misfortunes," or "The Black Fast."

I could see through time how the devil and his cohorts had attempted to annihilate the Jews, God's vessel to ultimately bring worldwide redemption. But I was reminded once again of God's faithfulness to His people, particularly today as we read the papers and see on our television sets the onslaught against the State of Israel. To me it was not a case of taking sides with the "goodies" against the "baddies," but more a case of stepping back and seeing the over-all picture and then reading God's Word and understanding what He says about it all.

I know God loves all mankind equally and has no favorites, so why in His Word does He seem to be so in favor of Israel when I know He loves the seed of Ishmael, (the Muslims) just as much? And why is the small and dusty city of Jerusalem such a place of contention?

I discovered that it's not a case of God having favorites, but it has to do with destiny and calling. The Jews were chosen by God to fulfill a purpose, not because they were any better or stronger than any other nation, but because in the beginning God made promises to Abraham, Isaac, and Jacob. In these promises, He committed Himself to be faithful and bring about salvation to the rest of the world through their seed.

This is what the struggle is all about as the enemy of God, the devil, has tried to destroy this process. Throughout history we can see how closely he has come to success, but then how God in His utter faithfulness has kept His promise of protection to the Jewish people.

Despite their continuous rebellion, we come to this point in time where we are on the brink of God turning the Jewish peoples' hearts back to Himself and revealing to them their Messiah. No political party or human being but the Messiah of Israel has the credentials and ability to bring about worldwide justice and peace. This is not a myth or Jewish or Christian legend, but a fact that is about to unfold before our very eyes in the not-so-distant future. God's Word (the Bible) is very clear about what is going to happen, and through today's media, we can see everything unfolding just as it was predicted.

If a person doesn't read the Word of God to find out about these things, they will have very little understanding of what's really going on, and just get depressed that the world appears to be heading towards chaos. People have no one to blame but themselves for having so little knowledge; the Word of God has always been there for each of us to read. But the Bible is the last book on earth that many people will turn to, even though it's God's personal love-letter to us, and like a manual, shows us how to live and what to expect before the end of the age. Most people have tragically discarded this Book of Life as old-fashioned or irrelevant, and in the process have shipwrecked their lives.

The fact that thousands of Jews from all over the globe are going back to Israel today in spite of the present attempts to liquidate her, is proof enough of the Living God. In the end He has one purpose at heart and that is to redeem the whole world from its pitiful state and, whether we like it or not, it is through the Jews and the Nation of Israel. God said that Jerusalem will be His capital from where His righteous laws and world justice will emanate, which is why there has always been such a fight for this city.

Aaron and I spoke about these things on the way to the synagogue to commemorate Tisha B'av. During the entire service, we just stared at each other across the synagogue while the service continued without us. The breaking of the fast that was to come had more than one meaning for Aaron and me—we knew it was also the breaking of our two-year long fast from each other!

After the solemn service, we were invited as honored guests to the rabbi's home, where Aaron would be hosted until we were married.

Once back at the rabbi's house and sitting around a table laden with delicious food, I felt so proud of my husband-to-be as my dear friends began to get to know him. I could tell that Aaron was far more than the rabbi had expected, and knew his heart was singing with delight. As he put it later, "It's wonderful having the honor of putting the cream of both crops together!"

We were elated, to say the least, and rounded off the evening by discussing the last few important days before the big day. We were to see lawyers and Jewish representatives to get all the legal documents ready for my immigration. Because of our unusual circumstances, the whole situation had, for the sake of convenience, been speeded up. Even before the final appointment came, all the documents that stated that I was a new immigrant were completed and signed. We were finding it hard to believe to what lengths everyone was going to help us be together. Further surprises came when we discovered the wonderful concessions given to a new immigrant. For example, the costs of giving birth to our first baby in Israel would be paid by the government and we would receive a substantial subsidy to help us buy a new home.

"What an asset I've turned out to be, after all the dramas of the past!" I joked to Aaron.

Then one of the most difficult tasks remained: Aaron had to do some serious, last minute shopping for something to wear to his own wedding. Being typically Orthodox and totally uninterested in the outer man, it was of absolutely no importance to him. It was a nightmare—trying to coax him out of electrical appliance stores and into clothes shops. This ended up as an exhausting, all-day affair where in the end we chose any old suit, purely because of a lack of precious time.

By then, most of my family had arrived and checked into the Arthur's Seat Hotel in Sea Point, where the reception was also to be held. It was difficult for anyone, let alone my family, to imagine that it was all finally happening. Elizabeth—their fun-loving, born-again daughter, sister, cousin—about to be married in a Shul! Even Mairi, one of my five wonderful sisters—who, pregnant with her second child (Jane)—risked flying. She definitely was not going to miss this one—come hell or break waters!

I still had to go through the last few but vital formalities before my conversion would be complete. This was my final oral test and an opportunity for the panel of rabbis, who would be deciding on whether or not to approve my conversion, to meet Aaron. It was scheduled at the rabbi's house on the Thursday morning before the upcoming Shabbat. Then to round it off, I would continue on to the *Mikveh,* where it would be sealed *forever.*

I would like to do a little explaining about the Mikveh, not only for my Gentile readers, but also for many of my Jewish readers, who don't know enough about this very interesting place, or its wonderfully symbolic significance.

In a new community, the Mikveh is the very first thing to be built, even before the place of worship. It's a place of cleansing, and way back during the Temple days, it was essential for the High Priests to go through it before meeting with God in the Holy of Holies.

The Mikveh is a body of water built so that the water flows and is not still, as in a cistern, being symbolic of living waters like a river or the sea, where the water is always running and fresh. A man-made Mikveh contains flowing water at least twice a person's body weight so that when immersed, the water acts like a burial, symbolizing the canceling out of your ego. You then rise up out of the water as a new person, like a rebirth, which is where the religious cliché—to be "born-again" comes from. That is why, in Yeshua's day, John the Baptist was immersing everyone in the Jordan River, urging the people to "Repent, for the Kingdom of God is at hand!" He was doing something that was quite normal and very Jewish, not something the Baptists thought of later as a good idea!

In a city, or where there are no rivers or sea, the Mikveh is the place a Jew would go for cleansing whether for their sins, or after childbirth, or even after a woman's monthly period. In my case, before becoming a proselyte, it was of great importance and to be one of my last ports of call before the wedding.

My previous submersion or baptism at the age of 21 into the New Covenant was a spiritual identification with the God of Israel through Messiah. Now I was prepared to be identified with Israel physically. I knew then why Rav Saul (Paul) wrote: *"There is one body (comprised of Jew and Gentile) and one Spirit—just as you were called to one hope when you were called— one Lord, one faith, one baptism, one God and Father of all, who is over all and through all and in all."*

I also discovered the reason why we do not have to repeat going under the waters of baptism (Mikveh) over and over again. Yeshua, the Living Word (is likened to water) has cleansed us once and for all, and He becomes our Mikveh. We are also then cleansed daily as we wash ourselves with the water of the written Word (the Bible), which in turn makes us into vessels out of which streams of living water will flow to bring life and cleansing to others. To me it was all so very logical and so amazingly beautiful. I could hardly take it in.

TWENTY-ONE

The time for Aaron to get to know my family was finally upon us. I dreaded this for no other reason than the fact that Aaron was so different from the average man, both Jew and Gentile. How on earth were the two worlds of Aaron and my South African family going to mix? We couldn't even share a meal together, "we" being kosher, and they—well! The impersonal hotel lounge of the Arthur's Seat was hardly conducive to a relaxed atmosphere.

We arrived a few minutes late for our appointment, due, largely, to me dragging my feet. I suddenly found a million and one things that I just *had* to do until Aaron called my bluff and told me I was stalling.

We finally got to the hotel and headed towards the lounge where my mom, Uncle Har, Grandmom Iris, two of my sisters, their offspring, and a handful of members of my extended family were gathered around a cluster of tables, drinking coffee.

"Oh, look, there they are!" chirped my mom, waving at us from across the room. Some of my relatives who hadn't seen me in a while tried to hide their surprise at my long, conservative skirt—well-befitting an Orthodox maiden, but in sharp contrast to my usual tight jeans and arty blouses.

Uncle Har stood up and reached out his hand. "Good to see you again, Aaron. How long has it been?"

"Nearly four years, I think, Harry. But a lot's changed since I first saw you, Rusty, and Elizabeth's grandmother in Israel."

"It certainly has, hasn't it, Mom?" said my mother to my grandmother Iris.

"What's that, Rust? Oh, yes, hello, Aaron, my boy. Who would have ever thought that we would meet again under *these* circumstances, hey?" She laughed quirkily, then scrutinized Aaron with a more critical eye than before. This was no ordinary Jewish boy; he was now the man who could father her great-grandchildren! Was the nose all right? Did his dark eyes meet her approval?

After a few moments, she gave him the thumbs up as she commented to my mother in a stage whisper, "He's got a strong face, Rust, and I *do* like his open smile!"

I groaned, audibly, but was chuffed that my fiancée had her approval.

"Come on, Iris, let the kids sit," said Uncle Har, pulling out a couple of chairs for Aaron and me.

Call me a coward, but I just couldn't bring myself to sit down with the family. Muttering something about needing to go to the powder room, I sped out of the lounge as quickly as I could, dragging my sister Mairi along with me and leaving poor Aaron to get to know my family on his own. "It wouldn't be too bad," I reassured myself, "he'd already met my parents and grandma before."

After a ridiculous amount of time in the hotel rest room, Mairi forced me back into the lounge, dreading what awaited me.

For a moment, I thought I must have stepped into an alternative universe, like in one of those "Armchair Thriller" TV shows. There sat my future husband with my little niece Sarah on his lap, happily chatting and laughing with my family about all the miraculous events that had finally brought us together. How could I have thought that my family would let me down and not make Aaron feel welcome? Oh, Lord, forgive me, and thank You!

"Ah, Liz, we thought you had got lost," said my mom. "Aaron was just telling us about where you'll live in Israel. Weren't you, Aaron?"

"Yes, I was. I was also saying that your parents should come and visit us as soon as they can," said Aaron lightly, as if he had known the whole family for years. And so it went on—Aaron answering questions and nodding his head sagely at little Sarah's jabbering, while I looked on in amazement.

At times, though, I had to wonder what was really going on in his head, and if there were any regrets. I mean, this world of my family compared to his was like chalk and cheese. My biggest worry was how Aaron would handle my very dear stepfather, Harry (may his soul rest in peace). Being a robust Australian, he obviously had some pretty lively adjectives, and I wondered how they would get on. Now and again I caught a shocked look flicker across Aaron's face at a number of flowery expressions that only Uncle Har could muster, but he just laughed at Harry's jokes and made the older man feel appreciated. That was the Aaron I loved—the gracious man who accepted people for who they were.

The longest and hardest laugh came when my stepdad began recalling the time when they had first heard about Aaron and the fact that he was "religious." He admitted that this had freaked him out, and by all the raving I did about Aaron, he was convinced I had met *the* Messiah! Aaron, embarrassed, joked back that he was certainly *no* Messiah.

But Aaron seemed to be really enjoying himself, loving every moment he spent with my eccentric family. What a man! What a family! I fell in love with them all, all over again.

The jam-packed days passed all too quickly, and Thursday morning came when we were scheduled to attend a final appointment at the chief rabbi's home. By the assurances given to me by the rabbi, I had nothing to fear. In his opinion, I was more than ready to take the final steps in conversion, and had no need for anxiety.

Even so, when I thought about how much was at stake, our future life together and the desire of my heart to finally become a Jewess, a wave of nausea washed over me. But the knot in my *kishkus* unraveled the minute I realized that Aaron was by my side. How could anything go wrong?

So together, we walked into that most-important meeting. There were four rabbis there instead of the three that I expected, but what did it matter? After the warm hand shakes amongst the men, we all sat down—the four rabbis on one side of the large desk and Aaron and I on the other. The atmosphere was pleasant and friendly, which helped me a lot.

The questioning started, and did not stop for half an hour. Their questions about general kosher laws and Jewish festivals I answered with ease, which calmed me completely as they nodded their approval. The more the questions came flying, the more I seemed to enjoy it. At one point, Aaron even interjected to defend me over a question that he thought was a bit unfair. But I amazed my future husband and all present by knowing the answer. I was on a roll, and loving it!

When all seemed to be said and done and every rabbi happy with the outcome, the Mikveh—my last port of call—was mentioned. Aaron leaned over and squeezed my hand out of absolute relief and joy. We had made it—we were home and dry!

We all stood up and started chatting about this and that, when unexpectedly we were told to sit again. My mentor, the rabbi, was the one to request this and he looked oddly pale and out of sorts. He said it was something quite out of the blue that he felt must be raised before continuing.

Not expecting anything major, I found it surprising to see that Aaron's expression had completely changed. What was going on? He darted me a desperate look, one that I had never seen before.

What on earth could be of such magnitude? What was going on? What had I missed? The silence was deafening until the rabbi finally spoke: "Elizabeth, I do not have to tell you how much I have grown to love and respect you. Having met Aaron, now I am doubly honored to see the two of you becoming one. Elizabeth, I have probably neglected to ask you this before, but being raised as a child in a Christian home, who is Jesus to you now? Is He just a prophet, or is He the Messiah? What is your belief on this subject?"

A bomb went off in my head. Aaron jumped up in my defense pointing desperately at a set of Law Books on the rabbi's bookshelf. He boldly demanded: "Rabbi, where in the *Halacha* does a convert have to say what their opinions or beliefs are about Jesus Christ? Is it not enough that she believes in the one God of Israel, the God of Abraham, Isaac, and Jacob? What has Jesus got to do with her wanting to live a Jewish lifestyle?"

Thoughtfully, the rabbis said that they had to admit that Aaron had a point and that there was no real law about this, but for now it was Elizabeth's question, not his. Speechless from disbelief, I just sat there in horror, paralyzed by this blinding question.

When it became clear that I wasn't going to give the answer they needed to hear immediately, pandemonium broke out, with Aaron and the rabbis loudly voicing their opinions. "What a mountainous problem! What on earth are we going to do at this late stage?" asked one rabbi. "Why has this not been dealt with before the wedding was arranged?" asked another. We were then asked to leave the room while an emergency meeting was held.

Aaron almost carried me into the hallway where the poor man tried his best to console me. Things were spinning out of control fast. Aaron frantically suggested that I tell an untruth just this once! After all, Peter in the Bible denied Yeshua, and was forgiven.

I didn't answer as he desperately tried to tell me that if I didn't come up with a satisfactory answer, all would be lost—forever!

Suddenly the door to the study opened and we were called back in. The rabbis had decided on a course of action. Three of them were clearly in shock as the other, my mentor, said, "Elizabeth you have got to understand that you cannot have Aaron and Jesus. You'll have to make *the choice!*"

TWENTY-TWO

The clock struck twelve. Four hours was all the grace I was given. Four hours to decide whether I would give up the love of my life or deny my Messiah.

I remember little from that moment on, apart from Aaron taking control and driving us back to my apartment. Aaron contacted my parents at the hotel to tell them what had happened.

"Oh, Aaron, I can't believe it! How is poor Elizabeth coping?" asked my mother in horror.

"Not well," said Aaron, watching me pace to and fro while maniacally gasping for breath. Three and a half hours to go.

A family meeting was urgently arranged in my parents' hotel room—but what could they do? It was my decision, not theirs. I was the one who had the power to change all of our lives in a few short hours—and time was running out.

But they arrived anyway, one by one, and gathered in small worried groups. Soon the small room was filled with confused relatives tossing out conflicting advice. I felt as if I was in a bell tower with hammers hitting me from this side and that. Eventually the clanging pain dulled and numbness set it. I stopped responding and Aaron became my spokesman as I sank back into the couch and stared straight ahead—I had become the living dead. Three hours to go.

Echoing somewhere in the background I heard money being mentioned—how could this wedding be messed up when it had already cost so much? "Especially for you, Aaron," said Job's comforter. At this unbelievable comment Aaron firmly retorted, "How dare anyone mention *money* at a time like this? Liz's life is at stake here!"

I wanted to die, or at best get away. Aaron sensed it. "Come on, Liz, let's get some air." He took me by the arm and half lifted me out of the room, past the gallery of anxious well-wishers.

Once on the streets of Sea Point, Aaron and I had to stop off at a shop. For what, I can't remember—who cares anyway! But it showed us how fast news travels. While floating around in the store, who should I see but my old friend Bella from the Shul. When she spotted me, the tears were already flowing down her aged cheeks as she grabbed hold of me and said, "Oh, Elizabeth, God told me that I would find you here." Holding up a packet, she said, "In here is your wedding present. You have to marry Aaron, because you cannot marry Jesus!" Bless her heart, but this was all too much for me, and I fled from the shop in hysterics. Two hours to go.

Aaron took me to the beachfront.

"Liz," he said, with a look as deep as the blackest hole, "you're going to have to do this on your own." I nodded. "Do you understand what I'm saying, Liz?" he said, holding me by the shoulders.

I nodded again.

"I'll go back to the rabbi's house, then you can join me there at four o'clock. Do you understand? Will you be able to drive?"

I nodded again, and then watched my love walk away, his shoulders stooped.

It was a cold wintry day and Sea Point hung in a depressing gloom. Lion's Head above me creaked under the weight of the sky and the sea was troubled. No prayer, no feelings, no thoughts.

An old man shuffled past walking his aged dog. The dog tossed me a curious stare as the man pulled his coat closer to keep out the biting air. Then I felt it, too—the icy fingers of despair, winding their way around my heart.

"I'll just kill myself," I thought, "But how?" Somewhere, deep down, I knew better.

More people passed on the other side of the street. Did anyone know, or even care what I had to do? Surely in this day and age of secular humanism, where anything goes, faith choices like this just did not exist anymore. God felt a million miles away. I stared into an abyss.

Don't ask me how, but slowly through the mist, thoughts of Jesus came to mind. I remembered how He had also faced a choice, a choice that seemed so unfair. By rights He was totally innocent, not deserving death on a cross, and in the Garden of Gethsemane the Father allowed Him to choose whether or not He would go through with it. "Oh, Father, if you are willing, take this cup from me. Yet, not my will, but yours be done," He cried, as drops of blood and sweat fell to the ground. Then He willingly laid down His life as atonement for the world, trusting His father to raise Him from the dead as He had promised. God never forced His will on His son, but He watched and waited to see Him obey.

Was He watching and waiting for me, too? Would there be any resurrection for me? Should I deny Yeshua, marry Aaron, and be "happy," or confess Yeshua as Messiah and lose my beloved forever? Would marrying Aaron under these circumstances bring fulfillment? Would my agony and pain of losing him be worth it? Could I or would I trust God? The choice was mine. One hour to go.

Time ticked by and the war continued to rage in my head. Jesus. Aaron. Jesus. Aaron. "Jesus, I can't take it anymore! Oh, God, let this cup pass from me, but Thy will be done, not mine!" Then the clock struck four.

Emotionally exhausted, I drove back to the rabbi's house. There through the frosted windows I could see Aaron and the family sitting in their favorite spot around the kitchen table. I was paralyzed with dread, not knowing how my legs were going to get me inside, until thankfully one of the young sons came outside and saw me sitting motionless in the car and called Aaron.

Just one look told him that I was in a bad way and in desperate need of support. As he helped me out of the car and into his arms, he assured me of his unconditional love.

He led me inside and I collapsed into the rabbi's wife's arms. She was equally distraught, and all the love and affection she poured over me set me off again. Eventually I was taken to a bedroom to be consoled. Then three rabbis arrived and waited in the study. One was missing. I learned much later that the whole saga had caused the missing rabbi so much distress that he said he did not want to be a part of watching a girl "sell her soul!"

My time was up. I was led before my judges who waited to hear my choice. They sat anxiously, clearly moved by what was about to happen and knowing only too well what devastating consequences my choice would bring—whatever it was. Aaron, as always, was with me, giving me strength. His loving face told me how badly he wanted to help, but we both knew that he couldn't.

Quietly I was asked to give my answer: "So now, Elizabeth, who is Jesus to you?"

I cleared my throat to speak, when unexpectedly an anointing fell upon me, and I found myself asking if I might go on my knees. A Holy boldness overtook me and in a loud, firm voice, with an authority that shocked even me, I heard myself saying, **"To me Jesus Christ is the Son of God! He is the one who died for me,"** then, pointing at the rabbis one by one, **"and for you and for you and for you. He is the Messiah. He was born of a virgin, and His blood cleanses all of our sins. This is** who I believe Jesus Christ is!" I then collapsed onto the floor in a sobbing heap.

The Lord my God was so tangible that my whole mouth tingled with pins and needles from the presence of His Holy Spirit. There and then, in spite of the pain, I was baptized afresh with His Presence and Peace in a measure never known before. He was clearly assuring me that I had made the right choice.

Bathing in this weird peace, I quietly sobbed as everyone else in the room sat in shocked silence, arrested too, it seemed, by the presence of this Holy God. I knew in my spirit that on this day, 'the God of Israel' had spoken. His Will had been done by His strength in me.

Aaron scooped me up into his arms and whispered in my ear, "You are truly the girl I thought you were and I'm so, so proud of you. I love you. I love you!"

The rabbi, who had asked me the fatal question, was clearly shaken, and, quite unlike the usual behaviour of a religious leader, could not help but grab and hug me, too, and say, "Elizabeth, the faith you have shown here today is something so great and so valuable. Does not Jesus Himself say that if you deny Him in front of men, He will deny you in front of the Father? You have done a noble thing, Elizabeth, and have great faith. Do you know that this is a wonderful gift from God?"

Then, to both Aaron and me he said, "Who knows what God has determined for you to do, Elizabeth? Maybe in time it is to go back into the Church and teach them of their Jewish roots." Now, years later, I believe that what he said was a prophecy from God Himself.

But then, in the trauma of my loss, I couldn't bear to hear it, and I flung myself into Aaron's arms and bellowed uncontrollably at the very thought. No words could console me. Yet, somewhere, in the shadow of my agony, there was still a strange yet holy peace.

TWENTY-THREE

My life had been canceled, and all because I believed in Yeshua! What about the countless others who convert? Some don't even know if there *is* a God—let alone the one of Israel—or have no faith in anything at all. Are all the "do's and don'ts" of Judaism going to help them in times of trouble or change them into better people? Why is Yeshua such an offense, when He is the very one who fulfills the Torah to its last detail?

"Abba Father," I cried out loud as I left the rabbi's study. "What we know is the truth. It's prophetic. This is what will happen when the Messiah comes. The two, Jew and Gentile, will become one. We are just ahead of our time. Oh, Lord, help them to see this!" But the rabbis didn't change their minds.

Oh, how Yeshua for all these centuries has been such a stumbling stone and offense, the "cornerstone" the builders rejected. Surely Rabbinical Judaism has tied a heavy stone around their own people's necks, a stone too heavy even for them, the rabbis, to bear. So, in one short afternoon all we had worked for was cancelled.

As they climbed into their cars, I knew these rabbis drove home, stunned by what they had experienced and wondering how this question of faith in Yeshua could have been overlooked. My friend, the rabbi, seemed no friend at the time, but deep down inside I knew that nothing would have happened unless allowed by the Almighty. I was furious, not with the rabbi, but with God! How dare He allow this to happen when I felt so sure that this was His plan for my life? He could have stopped it months ago, but why now, at the last minute? I was tormented with confusion and overwhelmed with anger.

The nightmare of all nightmares was upon me and everyone came to the rescue once more. A Valium or two softened the blow and it was left up to my family and friends to cancel everything and phone as many people as possible.

"Don't come on Sunday!" they were told.

"But why not? It's only three days away!"

"The wedding's been cancelled."

"What? Why?"

"Elizabeth couldn't convert."

"But why not? We thought it was all set!"

"We'll explain later. It's too complicated." Then the next stunned guest was called.

Through my sedated haze I saw my future wedding, my future life, being packed away. Serviettes were sent back, flowers donated to charities, the presents returned. I don't know what happened to my dress, my beautiful dress that I would have worn as I metamorphosed from a converted Jewish maiden to a fully Jewish wife. Like the white robes of baptism, I would have donned that dress to lay down my old life and take up my new. But now, it had to go. There would be no wedding. There would be no conversion.

Everyone said that they respected and admired me for my decision—but it had never crossed my mind. It wasn't I who had done it—it was His strength alone. I was just grateful for the deep knowledge of the truth inside, making it possible to do the impossible and choose something that was intangible over and above the tangible. "God, You must have some plan with all of this!"

It couldn't have been some sick joke played out to ruin our lives, as some people would think if they didn't know God's character. This is not what happens when you serve a God like mine. We are supposed to live by faith and not by sight, and boy, was this tested now!

That day in the rabbi's study, like a lamb on its way to being slain, I was, in my mind, already dead. Only the formalities had to be carried out. So, with nothing more left to lose, I had no fear of telling the truth, I just did not know how I was going to live without being with Aaron.

Many of the greatest truths in life have come from the lips of those who awaited the hangman's noose, or who have stood before a gas oven or the burning stake. But, with God's strength, we can do all things. You can never lose when you make a stand for what is true. It is always the hardest route, but the fruits of it are always life and peace in the end. The other route is always easier but guaranteed to lead to destruction. I'm afraid that's just the way it is. But that was not how I saw things then, at least not consciously.

The next day was Shabbat, the worst one I've ever lived through. There was no rest for me that day. I could not help thinking about how ecstatic I had been only twenty-four hours before. Now it was totally undone. Was this to be the pattern of my life?

While I struggled to keep sane during this day which was supposed to have been my last as a single woman, I just hung in there, while the rest of my non-Jewish family continued to contact as many of the invited guests as possible.

I overheard someone say down the phone, "But isn't she angry? I mean with *them*?" (meaning the rabbis.) But the strange thing was that I wasn't resentful at all towards them, even though this would have been healthy and normal.

My life was so much in God's care and control that I wondered more about *Him* and how He dared allow this. Surely, the God that I had grown to trust and love so much was not so vindictive? It was just not possible for Him to be like this. His Word says that He works all things together for the good of those who love Him. I was stumped as to how He was going to work this one out! How on earth could anything good come out of this horrendous mess? I was longing to know.

But I have to admit that I did not even want to know the good of it, if Aaron was not going to be a part of it.

I was scared of the outcome, not really trusting God with my future. Life without Aaron was impossible to imagine, so something had better happen, and it was God's responsibility to make sure it did. In spite of having stood for the truth, I felt cheated. Had I been fooled all this time, thinking I could trust Him? I began to feel sick inside because of the sudden doubts and fears about God's integrity.

This was the beginning of a crisis beyond explanation that was to take me to hell and back on that Shabbat day. I fought for my life as I swam in an overwhelming current of fear, doubts, and insidious lies. They swept through my mind, crushed my faith, and pulled me into an abyss so deep it almost completely drowned out the voice of life and hope. This was the devil at his best, trying to separate a child from the Father by fanning the waves of doubt. He was doing his job, and he was doing it well.

Then, within a split second, the tiniest spark of truth came back, giving me just enough time to see what was happening and catch my spiritual breath again. No, God was not unjust, unfair or unfaithful in any way! It's just that I could not see the bigger picture at that time. Yes, His ways are never our ways and His thoughts are not our thoughts, and I had nothing else to hold onto but trust.

Then, that same deep, supernatural peace that filled me in the rabbi's study started pervading my soul again. It was so much the opposite of my previous experience that I knew this was *my* God. "Please, Lord," I quickly prayed, "take these doubts and lies about You far away, and help me get out of this pit. Guard my mind, Lord, and give me the insight and shalom that come from trusting You!"

I remembered that somewhere in His Word He said that He would lead us by His Peace, which surpasses all understanding, into the truth. And He did.

While I was going through all of this, my friends and family gathered around me and gave me as much support as they could. My pain clouded out the shame and embarrassment, while everyone tried to grasp the reality and gravity of the situation. Never before had I experienced such love and tangible sorrow shared by all—Jew and Christian friend alike. Even though they didn't really know Aaron, they, too, seemed to be in love with him, and could not bear the thought that it was actually "over." There had to be another way around this disaster, and they were all going to help, no matter what. For them, and Aaron, this was not the end, but just a huge hiccup that would eventually be sorted out.

Now, with every door that had previously been wide open slammed in our faces, Aaron the "Israeli fighter" went into automatic pilot. For him it was just another obstacle to overcome and Plan B had to be made. So, with his hands tied here in South Africa, the next best thing was for him to return to Israel as soon as possible. He would continue our battle back home on familiar ground. Yes, parted again, but it was the only way out for us. Hopefully, with a little help from some friends, we would still win.

His top priority was to find a place in Israel for me to continue my conversion without the "J" word being mentioned. How he was going to accomplish this I didn't know, but the eternal optimist set off, convinced of future success.

The once thrilling "double" return ticket was exchanged for a solitary one, leaving us only five short days to still be together.

After many tearful family gatherings at the hotel to discuss what to do next, the obvious thing was for all to go back home and recover. The previous forty-eight hours of high drama had taken their toll on everyone, even though we still had a glimmer of hope in Aaron's abilities to turn everything around.

But no amount of encouragement from him did any good, even though I pretended it did. What was the matter with me when we had only five more days to be together?

With all the family and friends leaving and going their separate ways, Aaron and I decided to drive from Cape Town to East London, where my parents lived. From there, I would see Aaron off on his lone mission to Israel.

The trip from the Western to Eastern Cape along the Garden Route is one of the most beautiful drives in South Africa, skirting mountains, forests, and seas. But it all went unnoticed. It was on that ten-hour drive that Aaron, for the first time, allowed me to see and hear his broken heart. For most of the journey he uttered sad prayers in Hebrew as we both openly wept. He had been the one to carry, support, encourage, and never give up, but now was his chance to share the death and defeat that I felt. But then, his fighting spirit rose again as he started plotting out loud how he would continue our battle for survival.

"We can do it, Liz! Hashem will make a way!" said Aaron firmly, as he squeezed my hand.

I conjured up a weak smile. God forbid that Aaron knew what was going on in my head. We were seated so close together, yet our minds were so far apart. I just didn't share his hope. But I knew we loved each other beyond imagination, so why was I feeling this way? Surely love conquers all? And in my heart I felt married already. "I'm just tired," I thought. Yes, that was my problem and in time I would be fine. Aaron would find a way. I knew he would.

TWENTY-FOUR

The five days came and went. No matter how many times I tried to turn over the hourglass, the sand just kept on running and the day for Aaron's departure finally arrived. A chilly coastal morning added to the deep depression I felt, and I knew that the cold on the outside was more than matched by the icy chill of my heart. We were going to part again, but this time I feared that we would never come together again.

I was in no fit state to drive, but I refused my mom's suggestion that someone go with us. We needed to be totally alone, Aaron and I.

The little East London airport was small and dingy, and even with the freezing temperatures, didn't have an operational heating system. We carried Aaron's suitcases to the checkout counter to be weighed and tagged, knowing that our hearts must have weighed much more than the luggage on the scale. Other people noticed too, as I heard a lady say, "Oh shame, look at those poor children." Our distraught faces and body language spoke a thousand words, and people around us cast sympathetic glances our way.

Even though we were causing quite a stir, I didn't care if the whole world was watching. I clung to Aaron for dear life, frantically trying to draw strength from him, while trying to hear his words of hope. I was once again slipping into that horrible pit of emotional nothingness and Aaron was my only life-support.

The final boarding call shrieked through the air, ripping into my soul. I clung to Aaron even tighter, trying to absorb his words of hope through my body instead of just my ears. He eventually pried himself away from my pathetic, grasping form and forced himself to walk out to the plane. His figure became smaller and smaller, until I could take no more, and I turned and ran before the jet even took off. I wanted my last sight of him to be on the same soil that my body was standing on, and not suspended above the earth, like my heart. I staggered like a drunkard out of the airport building and let out an uncontrollable scream: my Aaron was gone! Gone again!

As I raced recklessly home, a sweet idea entered my head, and the more I thought about it, the sweeter it seemed: DEATH! No more pain. No more hurt. No more decisions. This must be the way! There was no hope for us, I knew—there was nothing left to live for.

I put my foot flat on the accelerator—enjoying for a few seconds relief at the thought of a fatal accident, finally freeing me from this pain. But suddenly, in my mind's eyes, I saw the devil—pitch black in appearance and smiling. He was spurring me on like a racehorse. A wave of nausea hit me at the very thought that this was his hideous intention for my life. How dare I give him that satisfaction! Reeling, I struggled to keep the speeding car under control and slowed down. "Oh, God, then You must have a purpose behind all of this. You must!"

The best place for me after this was bed. Like in a grave, I lay there for two weeks, hardly moving, let alone eating or talking.

Back in Israel, Aaron, poor soul, continued our struggle without me. Concerned about my state, he continually called, holding out all sorts of options for me to grasp hold of, many of which I barely understood:

"Perhaps we can have the Cape Town decision overturned." Or "Maybe if we go to one of the smaller towns, no one will have heard of you." Or "I might be able to challenge this at the Rabbinical Court—there's nothing in the law that says you mustn't believe in Yeshua. Or "We will just keep the Yeshua bit quiet, OK, and you can continue your conversion here."

Even his family was trying to help him after seeing the immense trauma he had endured in South Africa. Day and night he worked on different options, finding rabbis and others willing to help, and although it wasn't easy, he felt he was making progress.

Oh, how the war raged inside my heart and mind as each call came with another way around, his voice so hopeful and strong, desperate to strengthen me with his news.

"I think we might have it this time, Liz. I just need to speak to another few people." But deep down inside

I was screaming: *"Aaron, don't do this to me. I'm too tired. Just let me go, please!"* Subconsciously, I feared that it was over, but consciously, I could not accept the reality of never being with Aaron again.

Aaron wasn't the only person who called me during those dark times. Every day, at twelve noon, I received a call from my dear friend Debbie in Johannesburg. She would read the Scriptures to me and pour God's love and promised purposes for my life down the line. It was like life-giving water in a desert, and the miracle of hope started trickling back into my lifeless spirit.

My darling step-dad Harry was floored. Who was this woman, calling every day during peak rates? She must either own Telkom (South Africa's state telecommunications company), or be mad! Knowing some of my rather unusual friends, the latter was quite possible and after one and a half weeks of these calls, he was convinced that Debbie was one of my nut-case friends in a psychiatric hospital. Little did he know that she was my lifeline—she did not own Telkom and was definitely not mad, but a true friend in my time of need. Yes, Debs, you were an instrument in the hand of God. Thank you—you're probably still paying back the phone bill!

Then my mother—what a blessing! She seemed to share my pain as if it were her own and took it upon herself to help "us" live again. She could no longer see me lying there on that bed and she set to work and called the world to come to our aid. She had to do something, and she did!

Streams of precious people visited, prayed, and talked with me, but I was as good as dead and barely even noticed until one day I felt some warm strong hands enveloping mine. A tall, calm presence filled the room and like a Mother Teresa to a dying person, there was Eric Pike, the then Anglican Bishop of Port Elizabeth. His warm heart gushed forth words so sweet that I knew them to be words from my Shepherd and Lord—words of love, hope, purpose, destiny, and calling. Yes—calling!

A calling, even after all this—I had forgotten! He said that my deferred hope had made my heart so sick that I could not see any more reason to live. Correct! Anger, confusion and pain had drowned out the voice of God, and this was the pit in which I had been. True! He reminded me that it was a pit, not a grave, and that the way out was only if I looked up to the light—Yeshua—and trusted Him to help me climb out and find the calling that He had for me.

He also made me smile for the first time in ages when he suggested something so unexpected. He said: "Elizabeth, I believe you like jogging. Why not put on your sneakers and go for a nice long run? It will do you the world of good, and I bet you'll feel that life is not so bad after all!" What simple wisdom—and, it worked!

At first his suggestion gave me an idea that seemed even better: I could now just jog myself to death! Little did I know that jogging (or any exercise for that matter) releases chemicals in your body called endorphins that give you a boost. So I set off on my "fatal" run, only to turn back for home after a few kilometres, feeling a million times better. I felt for the first time that I could carry on with this thing called "life." With Bishop Pike's prayers and wise advice, I was through the worst, but still needed the strength to make more choices.

By this time Aaron had reached his final option for me and hoped that I would be able to make a decision within the next two weeks. He had finally managed to find three rabbis in Israel who were willing to interview me for conversion and weren't aware of my "shady" past. However, my belief in Yeshua was to be kept top secret.

"We can't take the risk that they may ask you about it again."

"But what if they do? I don't want to go through that again."

"Well, Liz, that's a decision you'll have to make."

"But I've already made it, Aaron."

"I know you have."

By now he was desperate and said that if I was unable to take this chance, we were to cut our losses forever. This sounded callous, but it was true wisdom. Strangely enough, as desperately sad as I was, that same mysterious God-given peace filtered through, helping me to trust Him to restore the broken pieces of our hearts and lives. I knew that the stand I had made for Yeshua was going to have to go full-term. He was now asking me, in a still, small voice, to willingly let go of everything for His name's sake.

In His Word it says: *Blessed are those who are not offended by Me!* Was I prepared to trust Him enough and not be offended by what He was asking from my life? Was I able to do this? No matter how unfair it looked on the outside? The choice was now my attitude: was I going to choose to become untrusting, offended, and cynical or choose to trust and be full of faith in my loving, all-knowing God?

To this day I will never know how I managed to cope with what was going on, but He did. He helped me every step of the way to stay sane, not lose my faith or become bitter. Anyone who has ever experienced something vaguely similar will know that fine cutting edge we humans operate on. I know for certain that without my Lord, a ward for the mentally disturbed would have been my lot.

That awesome Peace, which money cannot buy nor any pill give, is what saw me through. The ability to believe, in spite of my utter grief, that there is a bigger picture or plan behind it all, is nothing short of a miracle.

He has the right to allow anything or nothing to happen in our lives and it's all about how we react and respond to it. If we don't know His faithfulness and loving ways, we get bitter, resentful, and unforgiving of Him for allowing such a thing to happen to us. This is when the "cancer" sets in—causing deep-seated poisonous attitudes that can ruin our lives forever. It builds walls around our hearts and minds that shut out love, light, truth, and ultimate freedom, all because of the decision we make to not believe that God can only be good and make all things good in the end.

Always wanting to question can breed self-pity—a vicious hole to fall into. I wanted to be a person who stopped demanding answers from God and just trusted Him *completely*. I wanted to allow God to be God when that gift of amazing peace and God-given trust enveloped me, making the impossible possible. I was hushed and lulled into silence before my God.

It was inevitable that that unbearable final call from Aaron would come. "So, Liz, what are you going to do?"

Oh, God, what *was* I going to do? But I already knew—I had already made the choice. With parched mouth, I fumbled through words that sounded so trite, as I asked my love to let me go. "Aaron," I said, "I won't deny Yeshua, you know that, but what if they ask me to? I can't go through it again. I just don't have the fight in me anymore and I think it's a sign. I don't think it's doing us any good to drag this out. It's not that I don't love you anymore; it's *because* I love you. I've never loved you more than I do now, but I have to give you back to God. And I'll have to trust Him to ..."

I couldn't carry on anymore as I began to sob. Aaron didn't say anything. The separation I feared most in the world had already begun.

Between gut wrenching sobs I begged him to speak, "Oh, Aaron, say something, please! I can't begin to think of life without you and Israel, but what else can I do? Oh, God! Aaron! Say something, please understand, please, please ..."

Eventually Aaron spoke, but in a soft, deflated voice, like a soldier defeated in battle. "Yes, you are right, I understand."

The line was charged with emotion and thoughts of how or what to say next, when he asked me in such a loving and gentle tone to promise him something, "Liz, my love, we will have to cut this with a hot knife or else destroy each other. I trust you will honor this and we must then make no further contact. Do you understand me, my love?" The silence was eternal. Then, softly, he added, "Go well, my love!" Interrupted only by my pitiful sobs, we clung on for a while longer until I heard that devastating "click." He was gone. Aaron, my beloved, was gone forever.

TWENTY-FIVE

*T*hree tormenting months went by, and Grace was all I survived on. I kept going over the nightmarish events from every angle—turning each conversation, each action, each decision this way and that to see if I could have done it differently. I knew I had to stop this fast or I'd go crazy. No matter what the Bible said about God being trustworthy to lead us along the right paths, it all seemed too big for me and I needed God in a new measure. How was He going to help me trust Him when I felt so empty and undone inside? I needed Him to fill me and tie up all those loose ends.

One of them was dealing with my friends' many questions.

"Why doesn't Aaron just marry you like he said he would?" To their minds, if two people loved each other as we did, why not go to any lengths to be together?

Or "Why doesn't he just leave Israel and marry you here in a civil ceremony?"

This was totally out of the question as Aaron was not the type of man to abandon his responsibilities towards his beloved children. Then of course there was his loyalty towards Israel. For Aaron, his country was one of the main things he lived for, and after personally surviving two wars, nobody (not even I) could make him want to leave. Call it destiny if you like, but Aaron had to stay in Israel, and if I couldn't live with him there, then we had no future together.

But why God had allowed our relationship to go so far was still a mystery to me—if it had been called off earlier, it would not have been so devastating. I fully believed in God's love for me, but I was still confused; I had nowhere else to turn to but His Word.

There is a Scripture in Proverbs that says: *"Many are the plans of a man's heart but the Lord's counsel stands."* Also in Psalm 106 v 14-15 it says: *"In the desert they gave in to their craving, in the wasteland they put God to the test. So He gave them what they asked for, but sent leanness into their souls!"* And this I did not want! If I did not allow the death of my own will to take place and accept His, the price I would have to pay in the long run would be far greater. This is what I clung to—my present suffering was actually the better option.

This is the mystery of suffering for Him. The pain is inevitable, but not half as bad as the pain and suffering caused by our own willful choices.

We all know that in life pain is unavoidable, especially when love is involved. I was hurting like never before and I didn't understand why it had to happen this way, but I knew that one day He would show me the reason.

Even though I knew all of this, I still needed a small but regular dose of tranquilizers to keep the worst of the pain at bay. Even my breasts ached at times, like a mother longing for her suckling child. Most nights I lay writhing on my bed, yearning for my love, clinging to literally the last thread of what was his—a corduroy jacket. He had given it to me that awful day at the airport as a reminder and promise that he would be back. I could still smell him on it, and I imbibed it nightly like an addict on a fix.

Then, one night, I picked up the jacket and suddenly came to my senses. What kind of torture was I putting myself through? I had to get rid of it immediately.

My cousin Gillian was about to go to Israel for that year's Feast of Tabernacles, so I took the opportunity to send it with her. She would give it to my friend Bev at the Christian Embassy, who would then pass it on to Aaron for me. Not being able to resist the chance, I also wrote him my first and only letter since our break-up and slipped it into a pocket. Was he still as distraught as I was, or did men deal with these sorts of things differently? Perhaps for him it was business as usual, while here I was still in shreds! I just had to know.

Two weeks later a letter arrived for me from Bev. I ripped it open and ravaged the contents. I read and re-read those soothing words—yes, we still shared something, even if it was only our pain.

Bev told me blow by blow how the call to Aaron went. He was surprised to hear from her about me, particularly when she told him that I had returned his jacket. But when she mentioned that there was a letter too, he was there in a flash. She shared with me how after a short stay she saw him through her apartment window ripping the letter open and reading it like a thirsty man. Then for a long time afterwards he just sat in his car, staring ahead while occasionally wiping his face, telling her he was crying. That was all I wanted to know. Our love was real—it had not been a dream, and those taunting voices telling me that it had been a lie were immediately drowned out. Love had been and always would be in our hearts, even though physically it was all over.

But yes, the sun had set, and the day was over on this chapter of my life. I had come to terms with the fact that Aaron and I would never be together, but "why?" was still a question asked. This I knew the future would tell.

My priority now was to maintain a clear relationship between God and me and not to slip into that self-pity pit, guaranteed to cauterize any further growth. Unfortunately for me, I only knew this in theory and dismally lacked in the outworking of it. I found myself struggling to trust God and could still not see any value to my life. Not being able to be a part of Israel and the Jewish people anymore was unbearable. It was also beginning to affect my professional life. How was I as an artist going to paint Jerusalem and not feel great pain in my heart? It was then that I quietly decided to shut out this place called Jerusalem and Israel, when literally overnight, I experienced the most frightening phenomenon.

I was living in our family apartment in Cape Town, and had rented a small studio to continue my art. It was after this decision (not to paint Jerusalem) that I became very confused, and literally did not know in which hand to hold my paintbrush. It was as if I had lost all my artistic ability. I became physically withdrawn, unable to string sentences together, irritating my friends. This went on for a number of days. I cried out to God one morning, begging Him to show me what was going on. How was I going to survive without this gift? Did He want this, too?

Then, like an arrow to its mark, God answered. It came in the words of Psalm 137, v 4-6, written by an Israelite captive in Babylon:

"How can we sing the songs of the Lord while in a foreign land?

If I forget you, O Jerusalem

May my right hand forget its skill

May my tongue cling to the roof of my mouth

If I do not remember you

If I do not consider Jerusalem my highest joy"

I was guilty of forgetting Jerusalem out of fear of being hurt—my right hand had forgotten its skill and my tongue clung to the roof of my mouth. I realized how much God loves this city and that the love I had for her actually came from Him, too. It was my calling as a believer to love this city—in Psalm 122 it says that those who love Jerusalem must pray for her peace. This is a command from God Himself.

Instantaneously I was set free—I no longer felt as if my tongue was stuck, and the desire to paint Jerusalem returned with great gusto. The result was a solo exhibition, entitled, "Hear O Israel!" where most of the paintings in this book come from. I decided to depict prophecy to encourage God's people, the Jews, to read their very own Scriptures about the future of this amazing miracle, Israel. Through my art I reminded them that God has always protected and delivered them from their enemies and will continue to do so even in these very perilous times. God Himself is Israel's keeper and until they stop looking to other nations for help, or even relying only on their own military might for safety, and turn to the God of their forefathers for deliverance, there will be no solution and no peace in the Middle East.

As I write these words, the World Trade Center is now reduced to rubble, a catastrophe so overwhelming that we probably have little notion of how it will change all our lives in the future. I have no doubt in my mind that it is the beginning of a world shaking, of all that is false. It will eventually lead to all nations turning against Israel, either through Muslim Jihad or the pressure of world opinion, to try and force Israel to give up Jerusalem.

In the book of Zechariah chapter 12 verses 2-5, it says: *"I will make Jerusalem and Judah like a cup of poison to all the nearby nations that send their armies to surround Jerusalem. She will be a heavy stone burdening the world! And though all the nations of the earth unite in an attempt to move her, they will all be crushed. In that day, says the Lord, I will bewilder the armies drawn up against her, and make fools of them, for I will watch over the people of Judah, but blind all their enemies. And the clans of Judah shall say to themselves, 'The people of Jerusalem have found strength in the Lord of the armies of heaven, their God.'"*

From this and many other Scriptures of the Jewish Prophets, we can tell that ultimate victory will come from Heaven, bringing global peace and justice. No government or person has the solution to this problem in the Middle East (let alone in other parts of the world) but a Messiah from another Kingdom. We are warned though of the false ones who will come to deceive many into a false peace and security before the Truth, in all His Glory will appear.

In the book of Isaiah chapter 2 verses 3-5 it says: *"For in those days the world will be ruled from Jerusalem. The Lord will settle international disputes: all the nations will convert their weapons of war into implements of peace. Then at the last all wars will stop and all military training will end. O Israel, come, let us walk in the light of the Lord, and be obedient to His laws!"*

This is why there is such a fight for this piece of real estate that God, in His sovereignty, has chosen for Himself. It's just a matter of time before all this takes place and just watching the news is like seeing two-thousand-year-old prophesies fulfilled before our very eyes. God's Word clearly says that *never* will any army, even the armies of all the nations, ever destroy Jeusalem again. In the meanwhile God waits for His people Israel to cry out to Him in repentance and mercy as the predicted events are played out on the world stage.

But all of these events, including the destruction of the World Trade Center, were still in the future for me back in 1990. I had been unable to formally convert to Judaism, but I felt that it was acceptable to still be a part of the Jewish community, and in fact my very duty to stand by them, come what may. Although everyone knew now about my faith in Yeshua, it did not seem to matter a bit. I felt liberated, no longer having to watch my words or actions anymore. My story became the talk of dinner parties and coffee mornings, and time and time again the suggestion of writing a "book" came up.

I even remember when the rabbi once said, "Liz, your story makes *The Thornbirds* look like Mickey Mouse!" But being dyslexic, I did not even consider it.

I remember when my dear Jewish friend Karen and I met for coffee at *Riesies* in Sea Point. She was fed up with hearing all the rumors doing the dinner party circuit and wanted to hear for herself what actually happened. As we sat sipping coffee, I spoke and spoke, while she quietly wept at the horror of it all. She, like many others, had not realized the searing pain I was going through, yet marveled that there was no bitterness in my heart. She eventually could not contain herself and blurted out through the third paper napkin, sodden with her tears, "Lizzy doll, if you don't write a book, you're *crazy*!"

But I didn't, although I could never quite get it out of my mind. Then, five years later, the whole idea was stirred up again by the most exciting events that started in Rome. It happened like this …

TWENTY-SIX

It was now 1995 and the age-old fight was still raging in my heart. I hated hearing that God alone was all I needed—was it such a crime to want a husband? Surely God understood this and did not expect me to need Him *alone*, one that you can't touch or see! It seemed so unfair.

These feelings tore at my humanity and my natural womanly desires, blocking out the truth of the real cry of my starving spirit. I closed my ears to the words, "No Aaron, no Jerusalem, no Israel, no amount of Jewish living could satisfy quite like God could," and wouldn't listen to anyone who said it. How could they know anything of the love and lifestyle I had tasted? It seemed like nobody understood.

It was now eight years since I had been deported. Long enough, I thought, to be separated from the land that I loved. So, I couldn't have Aaron—did this mean that I couldn't have Israel either? I didn't think so. I had the *chutzpah* to ask for the go-ahead from the Israeli Consulate to return to the land for a ten-day visit. Writing, faxing, and phoning them constantly resulted in my being told that I would be welcomed back, and permission was granted. Wow, what a surprise—my mother's theory of "if you don't ask, you don't get," had worked. I was going home—even though it was for only ten days.

Coincidentally, my mom was also planning a trip then, to visit my sister Shelagh in Milan, Italy. So for company, we flew there together and I spent some time in Italy before setting off for my beloved Israel—I could barely contain my excitement!

My arrival was going to be on the eve of *Rosh Hashanah* and I had plans to stay with my long-lost kibbutz friend, a South African called Belinda, whom I hadn't seen since the early 1980s. Now she was living there, fully bilingual and overflowing with Israeli chutzpah.

Before leaving Italy, my dear mom had to spoil things by mentioning her reservations about my re-entry into the country. I was furious with her for planting the seeds of doubt that I fought from then on. Why did she have to mention it? Where was her faith? But what if she was right? No, out of the question! God had opened the door for me and I was stepping right through.

Finally, out of the plane window, I could see little Israel, painted orange by the setting sun—my eyes filled with tears from sheer joy. After a perfect landing and the usual round of applause from all the passengers, I descended the gang-way, greeted by a warm, evening breeze, loaded with the scent of orange blossom—a divine welcome to the land of milk and honey. I was back and in the seventh heaven.

Floating across the tarmac toward the terminal, I chose custom gate No. 10, the number of perfection, and prayed for a perfect entry. Giving a strikingly beautiful Israeli girl my passport, we greeted each other with the usual "Shalom-Shalom." Quickly she punched in the necessary data, then jabbed a look at me—for the normal identification, I thought. Then she asked with good old Israeli aggression: "When were you last in Israel?" Now my heart pounded uncontrollably, almost drowning out my nonchalant reply: "Oh, a long time back in ummm ... I think it was 1986."

Her expression changed completely and she pressed something under her desk. A shrill alarm pierced the air, and her aggressive face turned into a mask of steel.

My stomach turned to water as officials ran to and fro and the tourists behind me scurried off to other gates. As quick as lightning I was frisked and roughly questioned in Hebrew about things I just could not understand.

"I need a toilet, a toilet, *sherutim*," was all I heard myself desperately say. But a very angry policeman and his accomplices drilled on and on, believing I could speak Hebrew, before deciding to whisk me off someplace else for further interrogation, ignoring my frantic plea for a loo. Then my luggage was tipped out everywhere and searched until it, and I, were bundled off into the bowels of the airport building.

Although weak from fear, in a flashing moment I thought, "Good for them, because if Israel was not as vigilant as this, she probably would not be here today!"

But my altruism soon passed and I tried desperately in a smattering of broken Hebrew to convey to them that I was no threat—but to no avail. Unbelievably, I was still listed on their computers as a "security threat" and they were just doing their job.

We soon arrived in a part of the airport that was designed, I think, to drive one crazy. The noise, the fumes and the angry shouting, together with regular heat waves from the passing air traffic, hinted that things were not going to get better. Then, as we headed towards what looked like a holding cell, I realized that I was going nowhere that night but "JAIL!"

There was a change of the prison guard as we arrived and I discovered that the new one spoke good English with an American accent. I found out from this Godsend of a man that I was being detained until a flight became available for me to return to Italy! The fact that I was told back in South Africa that I could return to Israel made no difference now whatsoever. I began to feel faint and had to sit down.

The guard was surprisingly concerned, and I could hardly believe my ears when he asked where I was from and how he could help. He seemed to care. This was when I had the presence of mind to ask him to send somebody urgently to tell my friend Belinda what had happened. I could imagine her concern. She had spoken to me just a few hours before I left Milan and saw the plane land over an hour ago. She would be worried sick.

I asked the guard to tell her to return home where I could call her and explain my drama. With our New Year's Eve now destroyed, what could I say? I'm in prison, Bee—sorry I can't make the party!

Belinda, thank goodness, is the kind of friend we all need in life. Our time together in the Negev Desert assured me that she was perfect for the job—the solid, down-to-earth type, the sort you would definitely want on your side when at war. Her proven character over the years gave me confidence that somehow she would sort it all out.

An hour went by, giving her enough time to get back home, and I was allowed to make that one call. True to form, Belinda was there and ready for action. In a few very emotional minutes, I could not help but cry at hearing a familiar voice.

"Well, Liz, I hope they don't go as far as crucifying you! Nothing's changed around here for the last two thousand years, you know!"

After a good laugh, I gave her my sister's telephone number in Italy.

"What on earth can she do for you, Liz? Why don't we just call the South African Embassy here?"

Of course! I knew Bee would have the answer! She even convinced the "American" guard, (bless his heart) to allow her to call whenever necessary—another miracle.

With this done, I was shown to the "cell," a blindingly lit fluorescent box, about four meters square. Three dirty bunk beds ran along the walls, and aluminum food containers with moldy, half-eaten food piled in one corner told me there was definitely no room service. It was just like something in the movies. The smallness, stifling heat, and stale, smoky air got to me and I started to feel faint.

The only other inmate was a young Russian girl who spoke absolutely no English. With the help of creative sign language, I learned that she had been in this hole for the past seven days, which scared me stiff, wondering how long my stay would be! She was so thrilled to have company, that in a gesture of friendship, she generously offered me the last of her two cigarettes. Out of sheer politeness, I automatically reached forward and took one and we lit up. Being a non-smoker and a frustrated actress at times, I felt like a character in a novel or movie—"A Room with No View," perhaps.

There I was, sitting on the edge of a dirty bunk bed with elbows on knees like a typical jailbird, "ciggie" between my thumb and forefinger—I cracked into peals of laughter. "I wish my friends could see me now!" I thought. Here I was, locked in a jail cell in Israel, smoking some horrible tasting cigarette with a Russian who could not speak a word of English. It was bizarre!

Having to put the cigarettes out after the second puff, purely so that we could still see each other, my laughter turned into wild sobs. I cried and laughed myself into a dizzy slumber, but not before calling out loud, "God, where are You?"

After lying there for about an hour in this fuzzy kind of daze, I started focusing on the unbelievable graffiti covering the walls. Amongst all the fascinating languages, I finally spotted one in English and sat up to read. It went something like this: *"Don't despair, most followers of Jesus are imprisoned along life's journey, so cheer up, you're in good company!"* It was signed, *Rav Shaul* (Rabbi Paul).

This amused me no end when suddenly I felt the presence of the Lord surrounding me. It was like a light went on in my spirit and a supernatural joy started welling up inside. All I wanted to do was praise the Lord. I instantly knew that God was behind this and He wanted to talk to me. He had gone to extraordinary lengths to get my attention and now I was listening.

During this awesome time, I was shown by Hashem that no matter how special Israel, Jerusalem, and His people are, they must never become idols in my heart. He lovingly taught me that this is what had happened to me and it was not acceptable to Him. He wanted all of my heart for Himself before He would trust me with anything or anybody and it was He who chose this prison cell to teach me about the first commandment: *"Love the Lord your God with all your heart, soul, mind and strength."*

On top of this awesome discovery came the next heart shattering revelation. It was He all along, not only choosing this prison cell to teach me the first commandment, but "The Choice" of He made of *me* from the foundation of the world, and not the other way around. I had not chosen Him. He had chosen me!

I was overawed at the incredible scenario that He had put together to teach me this lesson. So much careful preparation and timing had gone into this and I felt like we were on a first date! He had reignited the flame in my romantic heart, which I thought had died when Aaron left me. I knew that from this day on, things would be different between us—the very God of the universe loved me and was wooing me!

TWENTY-SEVEN

*T*his euphoric state was abruptly interrupted when the cell door was flung open, and the most petite little Philippino girl stumbled into our cell. Seeing that she was frightened, I leaped up to comfort her. My arm so suddenly around her shoulder was unexpected and she pulled away. But my recent encounter with the supernatural must have been visible because when she looked into my eyes a little longer, she melted into my arms in a flood of tears.

We sat on the only other unoccupied bunk, which was shortly to become hers, as she told me in broken English how scared she was. After being shown loads of encouragement, she started to relax, as mother hen (me) settled her in. All I remember her saying over and over again, while looking around in horror, was, "Eez disgusting, eez disgusting!" Her name was Helga, and we became good friends, especially when I managed to give a contact phone number of hers to my friend Belinda.

Obviously I did not want the guard to know what I was doing (giving this number for Helga to Belinda) so we planned to speak *Afrikaans*—a Dutch hybrid and one of the official languages of South Africa. This was a real laugh, as I have never been good at the language, even at school! So when Belinda phoned again, there I was, trying without success trying to sound and look normal. I asked her in my broken Afrikaans if she could still remember a bit herself. To which she surprisingly responded in Afrikaans, "Oh, Liz, what must I do now?"

"Luister net," (just listen), I said, then proceeded to give her the number for Helga, the Phillipino, in such atrocious Afrikaans that we both started laughing hysterically. The guard was clearly not amused, but the constant blare of a loud TV, together with the continuous roar of trucks and airport traffic, thankfully drowned out most of our conversation. I think the irritation of his TV soapy being interrupted was more annoying to him than anything else.

Due to the time I was caught up in the supernatural, twenty-four hours had elapsed so fast that when a guard burst in and ordered me to get ready to leave, I was stunned. This totally threw Helga, and she jumped up in a flurry and said, "No, I go where she go. I go, too!" The two guards knew that she meant it, so after much heated discussion amongst themselves, she was allowed on my flight too, no longer going to Hong Kong, but suddenly off to Rome with me. How this was allowed, the Lord only knows!

We hurriedly got ourselves ready and I caught a glimpse of myself in a shard of cracked mirror—the past hours of agony followed by spiritual ecstasy had taken their toll. I looked like I had been mugged: eyes and face all puffy and red, yet grinning inanely from ear to ear. I was smiling because I was going home, yet more importantly from the beginnings of the new-found Love inside.

We said our goodbyes to the young Russian girl who was clearly sad to see us go, and hugged like long-lost buddies. It was dusk again and that same beautiful orange blossom smell filled the air. As I stepped out of the cell, I felt like I was emerging from a cocoon. I had gone in, feeling like a worm, but now I was a butterfly ready to stretch my wings. I felt so released that I did not really notice that we were climbing into a police van.

I also barely noticed the speed at which we were traveling. Just like in a Kojak movie, with wheels screeching and blue lights flashing, we came to a very abrupt and official halt at the gangway of an enormous *Alitalia* aircraft. The speed, the aggression, and serious looks on everybody's face seemed weird to me when I was feeling so good inside.

By this stage, all the other passengers were aboard and peering out of the windows to see who the people were that needed police escorts. Before their curious eyes, none other than wee Helga and I were bundled out of the van, with my unnecessary sunglasses on to hide my swollen eyes. I tried as calmly as possible to look cool while the whole crew of the plane, plus the two captains stood ready to receive their "criminals."

To cope, I pretended that I was royalty, and my acting skills again came in handy as I tried gracefully to ascend the gangway on very wobbly legs. The Israeli security was hot on our heels, and mumbled something to the captains who eventually agreed to let them on board too, to make sure we got strapped in and out of there.

By this stage, poor Helga was completely undone and unable to carry even her own hand luggage, turning me into a kind of pack horse, bumping my way down the narrowest and longest aisle imaginable. Everyone craned their necks to see what we looked like. Who were these girls that needed police escorts and why?

The sheer humiliation, embarrassment, and exhaustion made me feel quite dizzy. Once I was seated, I lolled my head back, closed my burning eyes, and prayed for sleep to take me. But my prayer was interrupted by a man on the opposite side of the aisle— his curiosity was killing him. Not being able to contain himself any longer, he bravely opened a conversation by asking: "That's a pretty accent you've got there, so where are you from?"

Looking into his very excited but nervous face, I knew he was desperate to know if I was really that dangerous! After all, I was seated right next to him! Every time I moved my legs or leaned forward, I noticed him flinch, as if a bomb or something would soon go off. Mustering up all my strength I decided to put him out of his misery and we started to chat.

His very strong American accent and loud voice reached at least the first two rows in front and behind, informing as many people as possible that things were actually okay! His name was Bob, and I discovered that he was the leader of a group of twenty-five members from a church in the States, who had been to Israel on pilgrimage. They were all fired up after their wonderful time in the Lord's land, and now this cloak and dagger scenario was the cherry on top of their already amazing cake. Much to my surprise, I regained a second wind and boy, did I give Bob and his friends their money's worth!

He could barely contain his excitement when I told him that I had just spent twenty-four hours in jail, but it became explosive when I told him that I was also a "Christian!" To him this was wonderful and after countless "Hallelujah's," he turned to his wife on the other side of him and exclaimed: *"WOW! Did you hear that, Honey? Hallelujah, Hallelujah!"* This was big-time news, and he got almost his whole tour group around my seat as I took them through my last twenty-four hours of heaven and hell.

Oh, how God refreshed me as I shared with those dear people the ways of our Lord! Like a newborn soul, I was free and whole, totally content to be going back home to South Africa via first Rome, then Milan. It was so good to be able to share everything that had just happened to me and there is very little on earth more infectious than a life changed by the Love of God. Although we did not know each other from a bar of soap, a unique oneness of spirit was there in a way only God can orchestrate. It was during that flight back to Rome that we all discovered again that it is not about *doing* for God, but about *being* with God, that matters.

While we were still in the swing of our excitement, the captain came down the aisle towards me. He was visibly shocked at the turn of events with me no longer the criminal, but now seemingly friends with everyone! I thought I was going to get into trouble for making such a din. He stopped right in front of my seat, with my passport in his hand, and told me to remain on board when we arrived in Rome. I asked why.

"I don'ta knowa why, Senora, but those are oura instructions from the authorities!" he barked in his thick Italian accent.

With that, Bob, my new friend, burst out with yet another loud *"Hallelujah!"* which woke Helga up. She, poor thing, had passed out like the dead shortly after take-off and had been totally oblivious to all the storytelling.

Bob was quick to remind me not to panic or feel ashamed, but to "rejoice!" I could not help but love his attitude—it was so typically American—turning my saga into a heroic tale. To be arrested *again*, in his opinion, was fabulous. Then came that suggestion again: "It'll make an incredible book, honey!"

When we arrived in Rome, all my new friends came to hug and kiss me goodbye, wishing me well in writing "it," as if it was a *fait accompli*. I was tickled pink, even though I was about to be arrested again and perhaps put in jail! I felt like a celebrity, when just a few hours back I was the scourge of the plane. God's ways are not our ways—they're far beyond our imagination!

Once everybody except Helga and I had disembarked, the "gang" waved to us through the windows and blew kisses as their bus trundled off to the terminal. Helga's eyes were like saucers, not believing a thing she had just witnessed. Who were all these people who seemed to know me and now that she came to think of it, who was I? She was dumbfounded. I had to smile as I took her small olive hand in reassurance, when the last words from my friend Bob were shouted from the tarmac: *"You'll be fine, Honey, and don't you feel bad now. We all love ya, and remember to send us a copy of that book!"*

We were the only two passengers left on board, and the cabin crew and captains waited for the Italian police to relieve them of their "prisoners." I wondered what outrageous stories they had conjured up in their minds—by the stony looks and flagrant disrespect, they must have thought we were scum. Our escorts arrived in two police cars—not so different from the ones in Israel—at a speed as fast and official. Blue lights flashing, with two cops per car, they jumped out and flew up the gangway to arrest their "criminals."

On seeing that we were females and scared ones at that, they kindly put their guns away and eased up. I think dear Helga helped because by then she was a trembling heap under my arm. For security measures, I think, they wanted us separated, believing we were traveling together. So we were whisked off down the gangway and into our individual police cars. Helga was in a flood of frightful tears as they physically took her away from me and I tried my best to tell the cops that she must go on to Hong Kong and not stay here in Italy. Whether they knew what I meant I don't know, but that was the last I ever saw of precious Helga, my wee prison friend.

I was duly rushed off in my own police car to the interrogation rooms where a very suave security officer sat behind a large, polished desk. A moustache dominated his face and from the bags under his brown eyes, I could see that he had already had a long night and was in no mood for trouble. The clock on the wall above his head read 11:30 p.m. It was probably half an hour before he knocked off, so he was in a hurry, but still serious and methodical.

With an owl-like stare he watched while the other cops dropped off my luggage and scurried out. Then he burst forth with a hail of machine-gun questions: "Why were you deported from Israel? Why have you come to Italy? How much money do you have? Why are you not married? (What that had to do with anything, I didn't know.) Where are you going to stay and what's their address? Do you have a return ticket and for when?" And so it went on. Suddenly his tired eyes were wide-awake and roving all over me, making me suspicious of some of his more personal questions. I couldn't believe that at a time like this, "it" was actually happening. But this *was* Italy, you know!

I answered as calmly and quickly as possible and was surprised to feel relaxed and in control. There was no fear whatsoever and I could tell that this man knew

I was innocent. He obviously trusted his intuition and with this, on top of realizing he was now officially off duty (being past 12), he came around the desk and true to form, proceeded to give me a big hug and kiss and welcomed me to Italy!

What a relief! After leaving the amorous official's office, I was immediately taken to the very late and last available flight bound for Milan to meet my frantic family. I was going home. Hallelujah!

TWENTY-EIGHT

*B*ack in Cape Town I decided that it was time to get on with my life. I was still nursing my shattered heart, but clearly God had put a big "no entry" sign over my attempts to return to Israel, and, of course, to be reconciled with Aaron.

I responded to an advertisement in a local paper for a position as a book designer with a publishing house, and miraculously, having no experience, got the job. I managed to hold it down, barely keeping my head above water in an industry that I knew nothing about. I was completely green, but I don't think my employers realized *how* green until I was sent on an errand to drop off a floppy disc with a printer. It was in an envelope and I didn't know what it looked like. When I reached the reception area I asked where I could find Floppy, because I had to put this on Floppy's desk!

Twelve months later I realized that the publishing industry wasn't for me. I was missing the Middle East and wanted to do something useful with my life. I applied to join Youth with a Mission, an international Christian organization that works in dozens of countries around the world. Finally an opportunity came up to work in Egypt, and even though it wasn't Israel, for me it was close enough.

My parents, of course, were horrified, half expecting me to get hitched to a smooth-talking Arab! They were grateful when a year later I came home with Egypt out of my system and my ring finger still bare. The Middle Eastern way of life has always been in my blood, so I enjoyed the lifestyle as well as the opportunity to do something useful—working in orphanages and with the poorest of the poor. But what I couldn't stand was the blatant anti-Semitism and hatred towards Israel. It was everywhere, even in the primary school across the road from where I lived.

Every morning for about half an hour, a child, no older than six, would holler through a megaphone and wait for his schoolmates to shout in response. One day I asked my Arabic-speaking colleague what they were saying and was horrified to hear that it was a death threat against Israel. The children were called "young heroes" and they were exhorted to shed their blood in Holy Jihad against the Jews because this was Allah's will for their lives.

That such hatred could be instilled at such an early age, and in a country that was officially at peace with Israel, appalled me. But it also reminded me of the devil's continuous plans to destroy God's people and the lengths he would go to achieve it. This utter ignorance of the truth because of indoctrination and religious fanaticism confirmed my call to help bring about the purposes of God by reminding people of His love for all men.

I decided that I needed to go back to Cape Town and continue working on my art while living out my "callings" to love God and my neighbor as myself, and to stand by the Jewish people come what may. Since then, I have been gainfully self-employed painting on commission and cartooning for publications. I never thought for a minute that I would be good enough to earn a living from my art, but God has blessed me with a gift and opened doors that I never thought would be open to me. The freedom is wonderful and it allows me time to do many other things (like writing this book) that a nine to five job would not allow me.

One of the things that I am able to do is still to be involved in projects for the local Jewish community. I never tried to convert to Judaism again, because I realized that as a born-again believer, I, as a Gentile, could not be more Jewish than I already am. As it says in Romans 2 verse 28-29: *"A man is not a Jew if he is only one outwardly, nor is circumcision merely outward and physical. No, a man is a Jew if he is one inwardly, and circumcision is circumcision of the heart—the Spirit, not by the written code."*

Inwardly, I am adopted into the house of Israel, so I have no need to convert outwardly. What I discovered about my Jewish roots when I met Aaron was invaluable, particularly the beauty of the faith when Yeshua is the focal point. Judaism, as God intended it to be, is a way of life with the many wonderful signposts (the festivals, convocations, and so on) that all point to God's redemption plan through Messiah. I still keep the Jewish calendar and its festivals, but not because I believe I will be saved through them, but because they are God's reminders to us of His love and His soon return. He *is* the Sabbath rest, He *is* the Passover Lamb, He *is* the living water of Succoth, He *is* Shavuot, the fulfillment of the Torah. But when the Written Word has led us to Yeshua, the Living Word, He by His Spirit takes precedence over everything—not breaking the Law, but fulfilling it.

Every day becomes Passover (deliverance), every day becomes the Shabbat (rest in Him), every day is Yom Kippur (as we allow Him by His Spirit to judge and search our hearts.) Every day I am consumed by Him because *He* is now my life, my Neshamah.

The Law was given by God to show us how weak we are and prove that *no one* can obey it in full. That's why in Jeremiah 31 verses 31-34 it says: *"The day will come when I will make a new covenant with the house of Israel and with the house of Judah. It will not be like the covenant I made with their forefathers when I took them out of Egypt, because they broke my covenant. No, I will put my law in their minds and write it on their hearts."*

When I fell in love with Aaron and wanted to be his wife, I saw no wrong in embracing Judaism as a way of life, as Jesus lived a Jewish lifestyle. But I never once thought that every Christian should convert, although understanding our Jewish roots will bring great richness to a believer's life.

There is a huge gap I believe in Church theology when it comes to Israel. Many ministers see Israel as a disobedient nation that had a chance, missed it, and has now been replaced by the Church. This is not what the Bible says. In Paul's letter to the Romans in Chapter 9, 10 and 11, we are told that if they (the Jews) do not persist in unbelief, they will be grafted back into God's tree because God is able to (Chapter 11 verse 23). Then in Chapter 11 verse 25 it declares that: *"Israel has experienced a hardening in part until the full number of the Gentiles have come in. And so all Israel will be saved."* I believe that we are now at the end of the Age of the Gentiles, and already God has started calling His children, the Jews, back to Himself where Gentile and Jew will finally be one.

Paul also warns the Gentiles who have come to faith in the Messiah of Israel "not to boast" (Romans 11:18) as *"you do not support the root, but the root supports you."* This is a truth that I try to communicate to the Church and take every opportunity I can to speak to people about it. If we are serving a Messiah who is from the house of Israel and the line of David, we had better get with God's world program and find out what our duties are as the adopted brothers and sisters of the commonwealth of Israel in these last days. When she, Israel, is under siege, we are, too, and this I am afraid is not understood by many Church leaders. If we are not for Israel, we are against her, and if you are against her, you might find yourself fighting against God!

If we, as the Church, are not hearing God's voice about His purposes and plans for worldwide redemption through the nation of Israel, or not educating the flock about their (the Jewish people's) influence in the Body of Messiah in these end times, I really wonder what Bible we are reading! The Bible says that our destinies are ONE, and which came first—the chicken or the egg?

So, my time with Aaron was not wasted, nor were the years I spent learning about the Jewish Way. I am eternally grateful to God for how I have been enriched by this incredible journey, having been left with one, but not the other.

After the dust settled and my life started getting back to normal, I asked my friends in Israel to keep an eye out for Aaron and let me know how he was doing. It wasn't very wise, but I was desperate for any news that would tell me that he was well. However, nobody saw him. It was as if he had vanished into thin air.

Then, thirteen years after I said goodbye to Aaron, I finally received news of him. I bumped into Sheila in the supermarket, the woman who was going to stand proxy with her husband for Aaron's parents at our wedding. We hadn't seen each other since those awful days after the marriage was called off. She delicately asked me if I had heard from Aaron, and I told her that I hadn't.

She anxiously pulled me and our shopping trolleys aside and said that she knew why. While my legs turned to instant jelly, I anticipated the worst as she proceeded to tell me. About a year and a half after the canceled wedding, she met a woman who had just returned from a wedding in Israel. The woman casually pulled out some photographs, and to Sheila's horror, the groom was Aaron. Playing dumb, Sheila asked the woman if she knew where the bride and groom were living. "In America," was the reply—apparently on some diplomatic assignment. To this day, I don't know who his new wife is or why he married her. Did he love her? Was it an arranged marriage to keep the authorities happy? I didn't know, but at last I had some closure and knew, without a doubt, that he would not be coming back.

While saying this, I don't want to give the impression that I have been waiting for him all these years. No, in time I started dating again, but have never married. I am a very normal woman who enjoys the company of the opposite sex and have had a few "boyfriends," and the odd proposal. But something, or someone, has kept me from saying, Yes. Until recently, I never understood why.

TWENTY-NINE

As I look back over this experience, I see stretches of time between milestones. Between these years, God has continued teaching me many lessons, and some of them I've taken longer to learn than others.

It has been fourteen years since my marriage was called off two days before the wedding. That was when I realized that God had another plan for my life, apart from Aaron, but what it was, I didn't have a clue.

It was eight years between my final parting with Aaron and my aborted return to Israel. That was when I first began to glimpse that Yeshua, and not Aaron, is the true lover of my soul, but it took another six years for that truth to sink from my head to my heart.

It has been six years since Bob the American shouted over the Roman tarmac that I should write a book. Finally I have had the courage to try. Those who know me will tell you how incapable I am—in the natural— to do anything like this, so the recurring idea of writing it all down had to be inspirational to say the least.

And the timing has finally come to fruition. I believe that the writing of this book needed to wait until I finally understood why God had prevented me from marrying Aaron, or, for that matter, anyone at all.

It was simple, but oh so hard to accept. The first commandment, to love the Lord my God with all my heart, soul, and mind had to become a reality in my life before I could go any further.

I now see His wisdom in keeping Mr. Right away from my door. He knew my heart and that the choice I had made all those years ago—to choose Jesus above Aaron—would be meaningless to me unless I truly made Him my all in every way. All this time I had not understood to what extent God really loved me and wanted me to respond to His invitation to take His hand and allow Him access to all areas of my life.

I know now that the experience in the jail cell was just another milestone in my journey with Him. God, the King of the Universe, wanted my heart all to Himself and He was hotly pursuing me like a jealous lover. He stood by over these years and watched me run after fickle lovers, patiently waiting for me to come to the end of my tether (not much different from how He is also patiently waiting for the nation of Israel).

The good that has come from this experience of personal weakness and disappointments was the very revelation that God wanted me to learn—to be humble and totally convinced that His Love alone is true and trustworthy. In the beginning it had been all about me, me, me, and what I wanted, but now it is all about Him and His love.

As I write, my heart is still tender from the sheer revelation that His loving persistence has converted me to obedience—which is now a pleasure and not a favor that I did for Him, like before. I have learned that if I do not obey out of love, I might as well not obey at all.

In the past, that kind of love for God seemed only for the giants of the faith and the drawing close to God and obedience thing, a total impossibility! But I chose to cling to the words of Love and the call of God to me in that Israeli jail cell. He alone was going to have to change and renew my cold and fickle heart or else I was doomed.

This is the point when I think He saw in my heart that finally I wanted Him just for Himself and not for what He could give me. Even though I still felt miles away from this ideal, I believed for the very first time that this closeness with God was not only for the mighty men and women of God, but also for the little "me's" and "you's" of this world. But what was the secret?

Slowly but surely precious friends together with wonderful timely books were sent as tools to unravel the mystery of God's love. Not until I was able to believe it and receive it could it become a reality to me. Soaking up their counsel, I was reduced to many a tear as I learned of their similar struggles. They too had come to a stage in their walk with God where there seemed to be a ceiling to their faith and love for Him. Like I did, they realized their utter helplessness and inability to love God naturally.

Another common thread was that they eventually had to "die to self." This was a laying down of their own egos, attempts and efforts, like a seed falling to the ground and dying. I realized that an exchange needed to take place: all of my life for all of His life. Was I prepared to do this?

I was once again faced with the choice, but this time it was not a challenge from a rabbi to choose between Aaron and Messiah, but whether or not I was prepared to take up the challenge of laying down my whole life. He had chosen me and given all for me, was I now going to choose Him and give my all for Him?

I realized for the first time the price paid by these other Jewish and Gentile champions of God through the centuries. They had died to self (their *Nefesh*, ego) and their reward was resurrection life (*Neshamah*). Yeshua, of course, is our greatest example of this. He laid down His life literally for the love of His Father, only to be raised to life again, the first to rise from the dead. Was I prepared to do the same? My response was a quiet but definite yes, as I counted the cost. But was I ready for the process?

I discovered that my heart was like an old attic, filled with hidden junk. Tightly shut drawers of undetected pride, offense, love of the world, lustful passions, and continuous idolatry came spilling out. Even after being a believer for so many years, could this be possible? More and more rubbish was revealed as Hashem's Holy Spirit did His sore but gentle "cleaning job" of my heart. I understood for the first time what it meant to be sanctified.

I realized, too, that no amount of my own charismatic talent or prayers of repentance could compare to a work done in my life by God. Only a circumcision of the heart not done by human hand, but by God Himself, would do. Of course, I kicked and screamed while it lasted, but look back on the experience now with deep appreciation of His loving and longsuffering persistence.

I understand now why God allowed me to experience a love so beautiful in the natural between Aaron and me. I understand, too, why He called me to sacrifice it. It was to show me how much more perfect and powerful His love can be. Perfect Love casts out all fear—after allowing this revelation to sink into my heart I no longer feared, doubted and fretted, longed, or sighed for things I felt I needed.

My future and the dreams that I still have, I now confidently entrust to Him who knows what's best for me, being so content in Him that I feel I need nothing else. A physical husband will be an added blessing, but not the object of my happiness, the age-old mistake we humans tend to make.

It is not by chance that you have come across this little book. If you are anything like I am, weak and in desperate need of love and purpose, you too need to ask Him into your heart. No one can meet your need better than He can. Life cruelly shows us that no achievement, person, or amount of money can fill that vacuum in your life, because, don't forget, it's reserved for our Almighty.

This book is a call to you from Hashem, like it was for me. He says to you: "Come to me, I choose you this day. I am waiting!"

No matter how wrong you have been in the past and no matter how many times you have chosen your own way above His, all this does not alter the fact that He still chooses you. God's love for us and His desire for our love in return are the very purposes for which He created us. He patiently waits for each and every one of us to surrender to His invitation of Love. If you are reading this book, it's not too late.

Strangely enough, all this has very little to do with religion and the man-made organizations that are in the world around us. But it has everything to do with a relationship between God and you alone. The organizations are tools to point the way but are not the way itself.

It is easily missed because it is just so simple and we seem to be programmed to think we have to do a million things to earn God's favor. This just isn't true. His saving grace is a gift that we receive by faith. Just believe and invite Him in.

His sovereign voice calls out now to those who will listen and He woos your heart to be one with His. You no longer have to be a lost soul, looking for meaning and purpose in life. The Redeemer of Israel and true Lover of your soul chooses you this day. Will you choose Him? The *choice* is yours!

The End

EPILOGUE

by Jamie Campbell

Truly, truly, I say unto you, that unless a grain of wheat falls into the earth and dies, it remains by itself ALONE, but if it dies, it bears much fruit. He who loves his life (soul) loses it: and he who hates his life in this world shall keep it to life Eternal (John 12: 24-25).

In February 2002, I received a call from a friend called Steff. He wanted me to help a girl named Elizabeth Robertson. Hoping I would read her manuscript called *The Choice* and advise her on how to move ahead and get it published. I am a manager for Lux Verbi's International Book Division.

My heart sank as it usually did when I contemplated the unpleasant task of telling another 'author' that the precious manuscript before me was real and inspired but unsuitable for the market out there that needed to buy it. But I took on the task for two reasons: firstly, I did not want to disappoint my friend Steff, and secondly, because the name Elizabeth Robertson rang a bell. Why I remember Elizabeth was because about seven years ago she came into my office with her close friend Trudi

Du Plessis, with this supposed same manuscript. Back then I told her to go and do some serious work on it before anyone would or could look at it. I did not have to guess at what thoughts went through her head at the time, so I was amazed that she now had the courage to come back to me of all people!

So reluctantly I agreed, but on one condition: supper would have to be part of the deal or no proofing from me. I told her that I needed a week to complete my side of the bargain, then we could have supper together and review the book.

The week vanished. I am one of those unfortunate single men that have the corporate disease "all work and no play," so our supper date was looming and I still had not read *The Choice*. It was Sunday night and our date was on Tuesday. "It's now or never," I thought, and started the book that would change my life. I was deeply touched by this incredible woman called Elizabeth Hayes Robertson, but much more by the God she served and the awesome way He used her. And I wept at the place where, when facing the rabbis, she fearlessly refused to deny Yeshua the Messiah at the most heart-rending of costs.

My mind flicked back two weeks to when I had first "really" met Elizabeth at Steff's place and recalled the magical walk we took together on the Blouberg beach. Before this day and because of circumstances in both of our lives, this woman had been veiled to me. But then, on that beach, I discovered that we had a multitude of similar interests, not least the fact that both of our fathers were Scotsmen! We even discovered that we had grown up on farms down the road from each other in the Queenstown district of the Eastern Cape and both could speak a bit of the native language, *isiXhosa*. But the cherry on the cake was when we started to play around on the beach and I threw a very high tennis ball at her, thinking that never in a million years would she ever catch it! Off she tore—skirt hitched up and legs bared—to catch the ball like a real cricket pro and throw it back to me! Her joy and fun-loving nature were infectious. Little did I know what had started that day, but I knew she was no run-of-the-mill woman and neither was this book.

By the time I read the book I could hardly wait for our dinner date on Tuesday evening and excitedly sent her an e-mail to find out if I could contribute anything to the meal. Ice cream? A bottle of wine? I received the prompt reply: "No, just yourself will be fine! Oh, and by the way, try to come earlier so we can watch the sunset down on the beach!" My heart began to race—it was as if she knew me already. Sunset walks on the beach were my kind of thing and here we were going to do it together on the first date. Something HUGE was happening here—I was in awe.

Arriving on time was another miracle after a hectic day. I had to drive an hour from the office, and arrived, a little flustered, to find Elizabeth ready and armed for our sunset walk with a picnic basket of note.

Another "coincidence" was that my father used to live at the very spot where Elizabeth lives: Saunders

Rocks in Bantry Bay. It was here that I used to come for holidays from boarding school in Queenstown. At the very same pool and beach where Elizabeth had planned to have our cheese and wine picnic, was where my dad had taught me how to swim when I was six, in 1957. Elizabeth was a reminder of my past and it was so special and nostalgic to return to my roots.

The sunset, of course, was beautiful beyond description and we spoke comfortably until it became quite chilly. I noticed that Elizabeth was getting cold, so being a gentleman, moved closer to offer some warmth. But then, somehow my elbow gave way and we fell into each other's arms to the accompaniment of a loud crashing of glass. My foot had hit the wine bottle and glasses and they hurtled over the ledge onto the rocks below! I had a flash thought of the Jewish custom at weddings when they crush a glass—"What did this mean for me?" I laughed to myself, "and with a bottle too!"

Back at the apartment and after a pasta supper, we put on some music. Then it hit me: this woman was just right for me. I took Elizabeth into my arms and asked her if she sensed what I was sensing: a tangible sense of God's delight in our relationship. She was in tears of agreement.

The next day was Wednesday, February 13th and I was facing my long one-hour trip to work that I usually use to think, plan, and pray. But this morning all I had on my mind was this amazing woman who had crept into my heart with such ease. I was elated—too elated to keep it to myself, so I called a very special and respected counselor and friend, Elizabeth Austin. I shared with her what had happened over the past few days and the impact it was having on both of our lives and how we felt God was very much involved in putting together something so beautiful. She told me that she was immediately aware in her spirit that God was the one giving this gift of love to us and a surge of joy filled my heart that had not been there for many years.

Between Elizabeth and me, we told three different people of our newfound love that day, unable to contain our delight. Strangely, all three people told us that we were to keep it to ourselves and not tell anyone. As we are both such open souls, this would be very hard. The next morning I was chatting to my secretary at work when suddenly it dawned on me: why would God tell three people to tell us not to say anything? It must mean He was saying that we were to be joined together as part of His purpose for our lives. The criterion I had always used to measure whether anything given or said to me was from God, was that it must be confirmed through two or three witnesses. And that's just what happened—flutters went through my stomach.

Valentine's Day, of all days, was now upon us. It was the first time in many years that I had a real, live Valentine to woo and I had to get creative fast! But nothing came to mind and with most restaurants fully booked, I called Elizabeth out of sheer desperation and asked her to pack our favorite picnic basket. I planned to meet her and then whisk her off to some romantic destination.

On my way there, a very odd thought flashed through my mind: "I want you to marry her." Marry her? Oh no, where did that come from? I dismissed it as one of those weird thoughts. But then, 10 km later it came back again. I turned up the radio, hoping to drown it out.

I finally arrived at the apartment and we ended up talking for ages, realizing too late that the sun had already set and there was definitely no picnic to be had. We boldly decided to test the odds and try to get a table at a beach restaurant in Hour Bay. With our contacts in 'High Places,' we did, and we sat there like two lovebirds. At the restaurant, I was once again completely overwhelmed by God's intense and tender love for Elizabeth. It brought tears to my eyes and as I told her what I was feeling, a question rose in my mind: "What can I do for you to prove how special you are to the Father and how much He adores you?" But what burst out was, "Elizabeth Hayes Robertson, will you marry me, James Maclachlan Louis Campbell, in Jerusalem?"

I will never ever forget her expression that night as the deep love of God's redemptive power surged through her. After all the pain, waiting and trust, it was at last to be given back to her. After dying and letting go of the right to ever have a husband and be loved physically again, the dead seed was about to be multiplied! I had no idea how significant it was to her that I was prepared to marry her in Jerusalem and how this would restore her dream of returning to her beloved city again. It was true that God knew her every dream and she had put Him first and now all else was being added. But this time it would be with a very different result, as God would give back all that the locust had tried to destroy and take away from her as the prophet Joel says in chapter 2:25.

Let's end this epilogue now with a brief look back to the last pages of *The Choice*. On page 203 Elizabeth says, "My future and the dreams that I still have, I now confidently entrust to Him who knows what's best for me, being so content in Him that I feel I need nothing else. A physical husband will be an added blessing but not the object of my happiness."

Elizabeth is a woman who dared to believe and trust God. What has now happened is a miracle of delightful proportions and we trust it will encourage you and whet your appetite to go in search of the Lord for yourself. I am honored to be the man God saw fit to love, nurture, and cherish Elizabeth, and to be used to give back to her what she gave to Him. Amen.

NEVER GIVE UP YOUR FAITH
AND NEVER STOP TRUSTING

"Who is that, coming up from the wilderness, leaning upon her beloved?" (Song of Songs 8:5)

A photograph of us on October 5, 2002—our wedding night.

GLOSSARY

Abba	Father
Chuppa	Wedding canopy
Chutzpa	Audacity
Gerim	Gentile who have joined themselves to Israel (like Ruth)
Gubbas	Friends
Halacha	The Jewish Law
Hashem	God
Kippa	Scull cap
Kishkus	Gut
Lekker Braai	Nice barbecue
Lo	No
Matzah	Unleavened bread
Mikveh	Ceremonial bath, a place of cleansing
Nefesh	Flesh
Neshama	Eternal Life
Nu?	So?
Oi vey	An exclamation of surprise
Pesach	Passover
Proselyte (Eng.)	Convert
Rak rega	Wait

Rav Shaul	Apostle Paul
Rosh Hashannah	Jewish New Year
Ruach Hakodesh	Holy Spirit
Sabba	Grandfather
Seder	Order. Refers to the meal that celebrates Passover
Sherut	Taxi
Shattel	Head covering in the form of a wig
Sherutim	Toilet
Shiksah	A Gentile woman
Shul	Synagogue
Slicha	I'm sorry, excuse me
Talmud	Talmud — This is a collection of books that are the normative view of Judaism as expressed by the majority of the Jewish Sages up until the year 500 C.E. It is authoritative and is the sole authentic basis of Jewish life even today.
Tenach	The Hebrew Bible, The Old Testament
Tish Ha ba Av	Day that mourns the destruction of the First and Second Temples and other calamities in Jewish history
Torah	The five books of Moses: Genesis, Exodus, Leviticus, Deuteronomy and Numbers
Yad La Hachaim	Anti-missionising group
Yeshua	Jesus (Hebrew meaning "Salvation")